Using ICT in Primary Sci

Using ICT in Primary Science Teaching

Jenny Byrne and Jane Sharp

Learning Matters

First published in 2002 by Learning Matters Ltd.

British Library Cataloguing in Publication Data
A CIP record for this book is available from the British Library.

ISBN 1 903300 40 1

Cover design by Topics – The Creative Partnership
Text design by Code 5 Design Associates Ltd
Project management by Deer Park Productions
Typeset by GCS, Leighton Buzzard
Printed and bound in Great Britain

Learning Matters Ltd
58 Wonford Road
Exeter EX2 4LQ
Tel: 01392 215560
Email: info@learningmatters.co.uk
www.learningmatters.co.uk

Contents

This book has been written to support primary teacher trainees and qualified teachers who wish to develop their knowledge and understanding of how Information and Communications Technology (ICT) can be used effectively in teaching and learning primary science. It has been written in accordance with the requirements of *Qualifying to Teach*, the professional Standards for Qualified Teacher Status, and clear links are identified. It also addresses the broader context of applying ICT by providing examples of teaching and learning primary science using ICT as well as the issues of managing ICT at different levels of school organisation. The book should also be useful to mentors, curriculum leaders, established teachers, those returning to the profession after a career break and other professionals working in education who wish to access a resource linking science and ICT.

The features of this book include:

* clear links to science and ICT in the National Curriculum for Key Stages 1 and 2;
* links to the Department for Education and Employment (DfEE), Qualifications and Curriculum Authority (QCA) schemes of work for science and ICT;
* information and classroom examples;
* practical tasks;
* links to pedagogy and different approaches to teaching and learning;
* information and advice about ICT resources;
* management of ICT within the context of primary science;
* further reading and references.

1 Using ICT in primary science teaching

What is Information and Communication Technology?

Information and communication technology is no longer just about the entry, storage, retrieval and manipulation of text, images, sounds and video in electronic format. It is also concerned with the sophisticated ways in which we access and transfer such information from computer to computer, person to person, right around the world and next door. Aspects of the Internet, including the World Wide Web, email and video conferencing, are influencing many aspects of our lives as we begin the 21st century. The technology itself will continue to develop and change, but ICT's real power in education lies in its use as a tool to support and enhance teaching and learning across the curriculum. Recently the focus has been almost exclusively on computers, but this book considers the full range of ICT provision and explores a wide range of opportunities to make purposeful use of ICT within the primary science classroom.

Why use Information and Communication Technology in primary science?

The use of technology as a learning tool is expanding as a global mechanism for enabling access to information and communication. It is not surprising, therefore, that there has been a slow but steady increase in the use of ICT in primary science lessons. However, the application of ICT in primary science is only now being fully explored. The most recent statistical survey of the use of ICT in schools in England (DfES, 2001) found that 50 per cent of primary schools were already making substantial use of ICT in science. Drawing together statistics from a range of sources, including Ofsted inspections and Key Stage 2 National Test results, the British Educational Communication and Technology agency (BECTa) has found that schools who have good ICT resources and are using them in the teaching of science are achieving higher standards (BECTa, 2001b). Whether you are training or already qualified, it is crucial that you are aware of the importance of children experiencing ICT in a worthwhile and meaningful manner within the context of the science being taught, and to consider how ICT will support that learning.

As well as using ICT as an aid to learning, teachers are increasingly making use of it as a medium to assist their teaching. Interactive whiteboards and large screens linked to a computer for whole-class teaching are becoming more common in primary classrooms. Word processing, graphics packages and data handling are all used regularly to prepare teaching materials and assist in such activities as assessment and report writing.

Reasons for the increased use of ICT in primary science

Statutory requirements

The National Curriculum
All schools in England must implement the National Curriculum. The latest version introduced in schools in September 2000 locates ICT within subject teaching and emphasises the use of technology to assist learning activities. The National Curriculum subject was renamed ICT to reflect the growth of importance of the communication aspects of technologies in schools. The implication for you, as a trainee or qualified teacher, is the expectation to plan for the use of ICT in your science lessons to facilitate the learning of science as well as to ensure progression in children's ICT capability.

Qualifying to Teach
It is a requirement of Initial Teacher Training courses in England that you need to be able to make judgements about when and when not to use ICT, to be able to evaluate different forms of ICT hardware and software and become confident and competent in the use of ICT (DfES, 2002). The Expected Outcomes of the NOF (New Opportunities Fund) ICT Training for in-service teachers contain similar requirements.

Global and local influences

In a world of expanding technology there is undoubtedly pressure to 'keep up' and there is an expectation from many of the stake holders in education – for example, parents, governors, LEAs (Local Education Authorities) and children – that ICT should be incorporated into all lessons including science. It is quite right that children should have the opportunity to learn to use ICT, as they will be expected to live and work in a world ever dominated by it.

Government influences

The use and incorporation of ICT as a learning tool is very high on the government's agenda. When the Labour government was elected in 1997 they committed themselves to 'transform education' through the use and application of ICT. These commitments appear in *Connecting the Learning Society* (DfEE, 1997), in which the government states its aim to create a society where ICT has permeated every aspect of education within ten years. The government has developed several initiatives to ensure that teachers and the children they teach utilise the potential of ICT. If you are training you need to be aware of these initiatives and what has occurred with regard to ICT recently in schools before you begin your school placements.

The National Grid for Learning
The aim of this initiative is to connect all schools through a 'mosaic of inter-connecting networks and education services based on the Internet' (DfEE, 1997). It is seen as a powerful mechanism for communication between government and schools, between schools and schools, for providing a wide range of learning activities for children and advice and teaching resources online for teachers.' See www.ngfl.gov.uk/index.htm

Schools will have had access to funding from the government via their LEA to purchase hardware to make this possible. LEA arrangements have varied and so you may well find different provision in schools depending on local policy.

NOF ICT training for teachers
Funding has been provided to train serving teachers to become more competent and confident in the use of ICT in their subject teaching. Teachers who have received the training should be capable of developing and expanding ICT applications in their science lessons. See www.nof.org.uk/ index.htm

Computers for teachers
Some teachers undertaking NOF training have been able to purchase subsidised desktop or laptop computers for personal use. Previous schemes, such as the Multimedia Portables for Teachers project have found that personal ownership/access to a computer has a significant effect on competence and competence with ICT and therefore on the integration of ICT into teaching and learning (BECTa, 1998). See http://cft.ngfl.gov.uk

Pedagogical and educational influences
Whilst the statutory requirements affect qualified teachers and trainees, it is worth reflecting that above all, the use of ICT within primary science lessons should be for sound educational reasons linked with your own approach to teaching science. Used well, ICT can enhance learning in science and so should be embraced and valued. Specific and detailed examples of how this enhancement can occur will be discussed at length in subsequent chapters.

Briefly, some of the benefits of using ICT in science lessons include helping children to:

- ask questions, predict and hypothesise;
- observe, measure, record and manipulate variables;
- interpret results and evaluate scientific evidence;
- explore alternatives, relationships, cause and effect and pattern prediction;
- present and communicate findings in a variety of ways, including offering a forum for discussion;
- consolidate and deepen scientific knowledge and understanding and to think scientifically;
- improve the accuracy and presentation of work.

In addition ICT provides opportunities to:

- model some of the ways scientists work;
- provide access to rich and varied source materials;
- speed up processes that would normally take time;
- allow safe access to difficult, costly or hazardous activities.

Conversely, science provides a particularly useful and appropriate vehicle for the meaningful use of ICT by allowing children to practise the four aspects of knowledge, skills and understanding identified in the National Curriculum for ICT at Key Stages 1 and 2. These are:

- finding things out;
- developing ideas and making things happen;
- exchanging and sharing information;
- reviewing, modifying and evaluating work as it progresses.

In addition ICT provides opportunities to learn in a variety of different ways and can provide an alternative or additional formats which children may find more accessible and relevant.

It is worth looking at some of the evidence for the utilisation of ICT in primary science before examining the principles that teachers need to apply when making use of ICT within their lessons. There are many long-term advocates of the use of ICT in primary science, such as Frost (1983) and Scaife and Wellington (1993). Heather Govier (1995) found that children using a multimedia CD-ROM to find out what they could tell about a mammal by its face were involved in a range of scientific thinking, including observing and classifying, formulating hypotheses and testing and refining them. Similarly Ofsted reports that the improved availability of CD-ROM material has provided children with valuable experience in the search for, retrieval and synthesis of data in textual and graphic form (1999). Willis (1998), working with children throughout the primary age phase, found that utilising datalogging in investigations, such as what is the effect of putting a coat on a snowman, enabled children to focus on the interpretation of data, rather than on collecting and recording it. She also reported that they wanted to try out many more investigations using the equipment: Ball (1999) describes a spreadsheet investigation with a Year 6 class of the effects of gravity on the different planets. He found that this strategy promoted high-level scientific thinking in at least some of the children's minds. However, preliminary findings from a wide-ranging longitudinal study on the impact of ICT on attainment, the ImpaCT2 project (BECTa, 2001a) suggests that when teachers use ICT in lessons they often focus on basic rather than higher-order thinking and reasoning skills. In a different study, by Wegerif and Dawes (1998), children were introduced to software that was designed to encourage exploratory talk about the requirements for plant growth. They found that improved learning occurred in subsequent science lessons for children who had used the software when compared to those who had not. It will be important to bear in mind research findings like these when considering the three Key Principles set out for the use of ICT in science by the Teacher Training Agency (1999).

The Key Principles

When and when not to use ICT

It is very important to think carefully about when and when not to use ICT; decisions should be based on whether the use of ICT supports good practice in teaching science. The correct use of ICT can undoubtedly provide additional learning experiences and enable children to develop their science knowledge and skills in a novel and dynamic manner. However, inappropriate use can have a negative effect, for instance by providing activities that are too easy or too difficult for the age and stage of development of the children concerned, thereby making children sceptical of the power of ICT as a learning tool. Alternatively ICT may be only available for children who have finished their 'proper work' and may therefore be seen as 'bolted on' and not a significant part of their learning; this also has the additional disadvantage that some children may never get to use the ICT available.

How ICT is directly related to science teaching and learning
This principle is applicable to any kind of teaching tool; for example, you wouldn't use a book that had nothing to do with the science topic being studied. This has not always been applied to the use of ICT; this is perhaps because teachers have felt that they are being driven to show that they are using ICT within their science lessons, and if some ICT is made use of they feel that they have achieved what is required. It is very important that you fully understand how the choice of ICT should underpin the science being learned, and that it is clearly related to the teaching objectives and learning outcomes of the lesson or sequence of lessons and fully integrated into your planning. The idea of some children not accessing ICT should not arise because if it is truly part of the learning experience then all children will have equal access to it.

How ICT can enhance learning by being able to achieve something that could not be achieved without it; or to learn more effectively and efficiently than could otherwise be achieved; or both
Within the science curriculum there are many opportunities to enhance the teaching and learning of science by making use of ICT, from using simulations and models when it would be impossible or too dangerous to undertake an investigation to using sensors to speed up an investigation. These and other benefits will be explored fully in later chapters. It is important, however, that if children can be provided with a first-hand experience then ICT should either not be used or should only be employed as an additional learning tool. ICT should never replace the opportunity for children to investigate for themselves. Children should not, for instance be denied the experience of building an electric circuit for themselves just because the school has some software that enables the children to build a virtual circuit on screen. Nothing can replace the handling of bulbs, wires and batteries to help children understand the nature of an electric circuit and why or why not the bulb lights up; nor can a computer package replace the look of sheer delight experienced by children when they succeed in getting the bulb to light or the buzzer to sound!

Links between science and ICT

Science provides an ideal context for the application of the four key aspects of the National Curriculum for ICT at Key Stages 1 and 2, (*Finding things out, Developing ideas and making things happen, Exchanging and sharing information* and *Reviewing, modifying and evaluating work as it progresses*) to enhance children's understanding of science as well as improving their ICT capability through practice. There are clear links between the requirements of the National Curriculum for Science and ICT at Key Stages 1 and 2 (DfEE/QCA, 1999). You will need to exploit these for the benefit of the children you are teaching. The programmes of study within the National Curriculum for science provide guidance indicating some possible opportunities to make these links. The programmes of study for science at Key Stages 1 and 2 require children to be taught specific skills and knowledge. There is an understanding that *Scientific enquiry* is to be taught through contexts taken from the sections on *Life and living processes*, *Materials and their properties* and *Physical processes*.

There is also an acknowledgement that learning science will promote specific scientific attitudes such as curiosity, respect for evidence, determination and creativity.

The programmes of study are summarised below.

Sc1: Scientific enquiry
* Ideas and evidence in science
* Investigative skills – planning, obtaining and presenting evidence, considering evidence and evaluating

Sc2: Life processes and living things
* Life processes
* Humans and other animals
* Green plants
* Variation and classification
* Living things in their environment

Sc3: Materials and their properties
* Grouping Materials
* Changing materials
* Separating mixtures of materials (Key Stage 2 only)

Sc4: Physical processes
* Electricity
* Forces and motion
* Light and sound
* The Earth and beyond (Key Stage 2 only)

The next section explores the links between science and ICT. Key scientific processes and subject knowledge will be discussed in connection with the four main aspects of the National Curriculum for ICT and the features of ICT.

Scientific enquiry

Planning
Planning involves children in a variety of decisions such as:

* what will be investigated;
* what questions are going to be asked;
* what the predicted outcome of an investigation is likely to be;
* how the information will be gathered;

- how it will be recorded and reported.

The key aspects of the National Curriculum for ICT, *Finding things out and Developing ideas and making things happen* make clear links with this part of children's science work. Children's ability to plan will be enhanced by the judicious use of ICT: for example, they may wish to access further information on the World Wide Web or via a CD-ROM or simulation.

Some advantages of using these applications are:

- to help children make a more informed judgement about what they are going to investigate;
- to help children to develop their ideas further in order to ask a more pertinent question to be investigated;
- to deepen scientific knowledge in both content and skills;
- to help children model how a scientist might work in the planning stages of an investigation;

The development of investigative skills in this manner enhances children's curiosity and creativity.

POINT TO REMEMBER!

You will have to understand and control the capacity and range of the information children will be accessing. For example, if the children are left to explore the Web without appropriately bookmarked websites, they may spend too long looking for information to the detriment of the task of planning their investigation and the use of ICT would not be profitable.

The provisional nature of ICT can be a useful adjunct to the planning stage of an investigation, making the link with ICT in *Reviewing, modifying and evaluating work as it progresses*. Children can use a word processing package to begin to write up work in a manner of their own choice or complete a prepared template. In either case, the use of ICT allows children to:

- make changes to their work before they decide what they will do without the untidiness of changes made to a written format;
- improve the content of their work;
- have increased confidence about making changes to their work.

POINT TO REMEMBER!

It is important to avoid using a word processing package to simply copy text that has already been written; this is not a useful activity for the children to be engaged in. You will have to decide whether the use of ICT at this point in the children's work will benefit what they are doing and enable you to meet your teaching objectives.

Obtaining and presenting evidence
Science can be considered, in part, to be about gathering factual evidence, and presenting that information in a particular way. This process involves a variety of skills such as:

- observation;
- measuring;
- recording data and information;
- researching information;

- presenting the information obtained in a report.

Obtaining evidence involves *Developing ideas and making things happen*. The children will be involved in gathering all kinds of data and the automatic functions and interactivity of ICT can be invaluable in assisting them in this process. Some of the advantages of using ICT in this way are:

- the immediacy, accuracy and ease of measurements from tools such as data logging sensors or digital measuring devices like stop clocks and light meters provide children with reliable readings, allowing them to concentrate on the interpretation of their findings rather than the mechanics of taking the measurements;
- the accuracy of the measurements also provides a better basis for children to understand the phenomena they are investigating;
- the ease with which readings can be made allows children to enter, store and manipulate data – for example, they may try out different sets of variables easily and quickly;
- children will be able to accomplish more in a given amount of time.

Children are more likely to *Develop their ideas and make things happen* more effectively by using ICT rather than more conventional measuring devices. The example below provides an illustration of these points.

CLASSROOM EXAMPLE

Children investigating why plants grow in particular places may use a light meter to gather accurate evidence of the light intensity in different parts of the school grounds. They can add this information to a spreadsheet and produce a graph quickly and easily to show the relationship between number of plants and light intensity. Children will be able to spend more time concentrating on interpreting the data and the scientific principles involved. Additional variables can be added easily, for instance data concerning the humidity of the soil or the temperature of the different areas. This will provide children with a larger amount of information to manipulate and help them develop a greater understanding of the optimum conditions for plant growth.

The skills of communication and handling information are paramount in presenting evidence accurately. ICT has an obvious link here with the key aspect of *Exchanging and sharing of information*. ICT can be employed successfully to handle data by using spreadsheets, databases and graphing packages. The range and capacity of electronic sources to assist research for additional factual information, access previously stored data and add to that data will extend children's knowledge, provide them with an understanding of how scientists work at particular times and help to develop their creativity and curiosity. Children will need to become accustomed to sharing information and presenting evidence in a variety of formats. ICT provides an ideal mechanism to present text, charts, diagrams, graphs; for example, children could use a table to present their results when investigating the stretch of a spring and the masses added to it and a line graph to show the relationship between the two variables, whilst a bar chart would be a useful way of presenting the number of different plants found on the school field. Children will therefore be involved in *reviewing, modifying and evaluating work as it progresses* at this point, to decide how best to present their results.

Children can benefit by making use of key features of ICT such as capacity and range, provisionality and interactivity, to edit text on screen and change graphs easily and simply, in order to present ideas and data in the most appropriate format for their particular audience. For example, children working on the topic of 'Myself' will gather a variety of data about the children in the class; this may include:

- height;
- eye colour;
- hair colour;
- shoe size;
- hand span.

They will need to consider the best way of presenting this data; for example, a bar chart for shoe size, a histogram for height, a pie chart for eye colour and a scattergram if they were investigating the relationship between shoe size and height. ICT allows children to present their data and, if they have chosen inappropriately, changes can be made swiftly and easily. Children may have represented the heights of the group as a bar chart rather than as a histogram, and a pictogram rather than a bar chart may be more appropriate for younger children.

Word processing, presentation software, overhead projectors and graphics programs can all assist in the succinct and meaningful presentation of the evidence obtained. The range and variety of ICT applications at children's disposal to enable them to relay the information to an audience is highly likely to enhance their communication skills and their creativity.

POINT TO REMEMBER!

It is important for you to decide if the use of ICT will enhance children's learning and whether your teaching objectives would be facilitated by employing ICT. If you want children to learn how to use a thermometer and be able to read it, then employing data logging sensors would clearly not allow your teaching objectives to be met.

Considering evidence and evaluating

Collecting and presenting useful data in science allows children to interpret their results in a meaningful manner. Considering and evaluating evidence involves:

- making sense of findings;
- providing meaningful explanations;
- considering what can be done to improve the work;
- considering what further questions they might be asked.

ICT can be useful in providing the means to:

- interpret results;
- evaluate scientific evidence;
- explore alternatives, relationships, cause and effect and pattern prediction.

Making use of databases, spreadsheets and graphing programs to consider and evaluate science work helps children to *develop ideas and make things happen*. Children can see patterns emerge from the data quickly; the immediate effects of change can be explored using formulae within a spreadsheet, providing children with the chance to explore and model alternatives. Children investigating the relationship between mass of an object and friction can enter their data into a spreadsheet and model the effect of increasing the mass systematically.

The provisionality and interactivity of ICT allows children to concentrate on *what* has happened, and *why* it has happened, which encourages higher-order thinking skills. Children's science knowledge will be clearly enhanced by this process. Children's curiosity is also stimulated as a result of employing these applications by enabling them to ask the 'I wonder what will happen if…' type of question.

Reviewing, modifying and evaluating work as it progresses is an important aspect of this part of children's work in science. Children will not only be able to interpret their findings but also consider what alternatives might be possible. They also have the opportunity to exchange results easily with other members of the class through a computer network or with children in another school through email. Armed with a range of evidence from their own work and that of others they will be in a good position to evaluate their work.

Subject knowledge
When the key aspects of the National Curriculum for ICT are employed appropriately, children's science subject knowledge and understanding is extended and developed. Children using science-rich sources of information – for example, a CD-ROM – will be *Finding things out*. This will assist them in knowing and understanding particular facts and concepts in science – for example, the nature of the atmosphere of particular planets or the functioning of the heart. Preparing a report using a word processor will involve *Reviewing, modifying and evaluating work as it progresses*; this will develop understanding of how scientists present information and consolidate their knowledge of the report's contents. When children make use of databases, models and simulations, they are extending their subject knowledge and understanding of science-specific content as well as key skills by *Developing ideas and making things happen and exchanging and sharing information*. The preceding paragraphs have discussed these and other examples and acknowledged that subject-specific contexts provide the vehicle for teaching scientific enquiry.

In conclusion
This chapter has sought to identify various and sometimes conflicting reasons for making use of ICT within primary science lessons. There is a potential danger of applying ICT as a 'good thing' without thinking through the application. The ICT tools at your disposal can clearly assist children in developing the thinking skills, knowledge and attitudes required of a scientist. By engaging with ICT in meaningful contexts, children will gain useful knowledge and skills with regard not only to their science learning but also to their ICT capability. As trainees or established teachers, you will need

to provide opportunities for children to make use of ICT within science and also be able to justify why you are using it whilst indicating the links with the ICT National Curriculum. It is important that you have a clear view of the extensive situations in which ICT can be employed in science and that you make the links overt for the children and yourself.

Finally, the important thing to remember is that ICT can be a useful and powerful resource to aid learning and assist in the effective teaching of science. It is this aspect that must be in the forefront of your minds when you are making decisions about its application in the primary science classroom.

FURTHER READING
Computers for Teachers: http://cft.ngfl.gov.uk/
National Grid for Learning : www.ngfl.gov.uk/index.html
New Opportunities Fund: www.nof.org.uk/index.htm
TTA (1999) *Using information and communications technology to meet teaching objectives in science: primary.* London: TTA.

2 Self-evaluation of needs

This chapter is intended to provide you with an opportunity to begin to recognise your strengths and needs with respect to ICT and science teaching. The self-evaluation exercise presented is based upon the Professional Standards for Qualified Teacher Status, Qualifying to Teach (DfES 2002) and its accompanying handbook. It may also be a useful guide for established teachers and those returning to the profession after a career break. Undertaking this simple self-evaluation will allow you to gauge your level of competence and give you an indication of the areas you will need to concentrate on. It will allow you to set some targets for improvement, whatever point of your career you have reached. Reading this book and undertaking the tasks at the end of Chapters 3 and 4 will help you towards achieving your targets.

Self-evaluation exercise

Please respond to the following statements honestly. Do not worry too much if you find that you are unable to provide evidence or think of examples for each statement. You can revisit the exercise at any time to check your progress. You will have plenty of time on your course or in your daily practice to remedy particular areas.

Identifying teaching objectives

Reasons for using ICT
When you are planning a sequence of science lessons and identifying teaching objectives do you consider when the use of ICT can be beneficial to assist in meeting those objectives?

In particular do you consider how:

- the speed and automatic functions of ICT allows you to achieve teaching objectives more effectively, e.g. using data logging equipment to measure the light intensity of different parts of the classroom;
- the capacity and range of ICT can enable you and the children to gain access to information quickly and easily e.g. by using a CD-ROM or the World Wide Web;
- the provisional nature of information stored allows children to change and alter work easily e.g. editing text, altering the presentation of data;
- the interactivity of ICT allows children to develop their ideas and relate to information or other people e.g. using email or modelling events from previously collected data?

Reasons for not using ICT
When you are planning a sequence of science lessons and identify the teaching objectives do you consider when the use of ICT may sometimes hinder meeting those objectives?

In particular, do you consider how:

- the development of particular skills which are part of your objectives may be inhibited by using ICT, e.g. producing a graph or observational drawing;
- focus may be drawn away from the science being taught by using ICT to undertake simple or routine tasks, e.g. using a light gate rather than a stopwatch to time events if very accurate timings are not required;
- using complicated equipment can be time consuming, e.g. making a video recording to gather results of an investigation;
- enhancing the presentation of work using ICT can be inappropriate, e.g. typing up an account of an investigation?

Planning
When you are planning to use ICT in your lessons do you identify the benefits that will accrue from its use?

In particular, do you consider:

- how and why ICT will be used to achieve the teaching and learning objectives;
- key questions and ideas to ensure appropriate intervention to focus and extend children's learning, e.g. when children are using datalogging equipment you intervene to ensure they can interpret the graph produced with understanding;
- specific tasks and activities to enable children to achieve the teaching and learning objectives e.g. identifying particular facts from a CD-ROM, providing structured questions to use when visiting a website;
- what resources are appropriate for particular tasks and children, e.g. suitable equipment, content of CD-ROMs, identifying and book marking suitable websites;
- how ICT can assist children with special educational needs, e.g. recording information on an audio tape rather than writing it down, and the use of overlay keyboards;
- ways of developing children's work beyond the lesson, e.g. through homework clubs, or allowing children to complete work at home;
- how using ICT in a science context can assist specific ICT capability, e.g. the use of appropriate terminology, and specific IT skills?

Organisation and management
When you make use of ICT do you recognise its impact on the organisation and management of the lesson and the benefits of employing specific strategies?

In particular, do you consider:

- the use of whole class demonstration as part of your teaching when appropriate, e.g. when introducing a new topic by using an electronic whiteboard or single screen;
- making use of group, paired and individual working to ensure children are engaged in the work, e.g. giving specific tasks to different children when they are working at the computer;

- allowing access to ICT resources as part of planned and spontaneous need, e.g. for research purposes;
- making use of equipment to its best advantage, e.g. portable data-logging equipment, digital cameras to gather data during field work;
- managing a computer suite to ensure individual, paired, group and whole class teaching occurs;
- how to make best use of space and other adult support e.g. having space beside the computer to carry out an investigation, positioning computers to avoid other children becoming distracted, employing a teaching assistant to help children with complex equipment;
- health and safety issues?

Monitoring and assessment
When you use ICT in science lessons do you determine how you will monitor and assess children?

In particular, do you:

- identify assessment criteria based upon the teaching and learning objectives in your planning;
- intervene at appropriate times to question children and to support learning;
- ensure you can assess what science is understood e.g. can children interpret graphs and not just produce them from a software program;
- consider how you will assess individuals if they have been working as a group e.g. asking individual children for a summary of the work undertaken?

Personal use
Do you make use of ICT to enhance your teaching and improve your professional efficiency?

In particular, do you use ICT to:

- aid administration, record keeping, reporting and transfer of information;
- prepare teaching and learning resources;
- join in professional discussions, and locate and access teaching plans and other material and sources of help;
- assist in your continuing professional development?

Reflection

Having completed your self-evaluation exercise you will need to review your responses and identify key areas for improvement. You should then set specific targets that you feel are focused, achievable and time bonded. Using the table provided, prepare an action plan to assist you in setting out your targets, monitoring their progress and ensuring that you are not trying to do too much all at once. You may wish to set yourself two or three targets for this half term and monitor your progress towards achieving them. Then you can return to your self-evaluation to set some more targets.

Areas for Improvement	Targets	Action	Time
E.g. Planning	To be confident in deciding how and when ICT can be used to achieve teaching and learning objectives	• Read Chapters 3 and 4 of this book • Look at the school's science scheme of work and medium-term plan for the upcoming half term • Identify opportunities where ICT would be effective in achieving teaching and learning objectives • Amend planning to incorporate these	3 March 10 March

FURTHER READING

DfEE/QCA (1999) *The National Curriculum: Handbook for Primary Teachers in England*. London: DfEE.

DfES (2002) *Qualifying to Teach: Professional Standards for Qualified Teacher Status and Requirements for Intitial Teacher Training*. London: DfEE.

QCA (1998a) *A Scheme of Work for Key Stages 1 and 2: Science*. London: QCA.

QCA (1998b) *A Scheme of Work for Key Stages 1 and 2: ICT*. London: QCA.

TTA (1999) *Using information and communications technology to meet teaching objectives in science: primary*. London: TTA.

3 Using computers in primary science

This chapter will explore the use of computers to enhance the teaching and learning of primary science. The purpose of the chapter is to provide a framework and guidance for the effective use of computers in science lessons. The chapter will provide a brief explanation of the different applications of computer technology. It will indicate how each application can facilitate science skills, knowledge and attitudes. Classroom teaching scenarios are used to exemplify these applications in primary science. These activities relate to all aspects of the programmes of study at Key Stages 1 and 2 for science and ICT. For trainee teachers, teaching these examples or similar lessons will help you fulfil the requirements of *Qualifying to Teach* (DfES, 2002), the professional standard for qualified teacher status. Two tasks are also included to help you familiarise yourself with the requirements and work towards meeting them.

Further examples and detailed information about ICT resources for primary science are presented in Chapter 6 and the Appendix.

The aspects of computer technology that can enhance children's knowledge, understanding, skills and attitudes in primary science are:

- data handling;
- sensors and data logging;
- electronic information sources;
- control technology;
- communications technology;
- simulation and modelling;
- publication and presentation software.

Data handling

Science is in part about making use of information regarding specific events or phenomena. The information has to be collected, recorded and managed in some way. Handling data is therefore an important part of science. ICT provides a useful and welcome addition to the instruments at the disposal of scientists to manage their data. Children should be able to decide what information they wish to gather, collect, record and store, and be able to retrieve and interrogate the stored information to make comparisons and identify trends. These processes can involve children in using databases and spreadsheets as well as graphing programs.

Presentation of data
There are three main types of data:

- *categorical* – the information falls into distinct qualitative categories, e.g. eye colour or leaf shape, that do not overlap in any way;

- *discrete* – the information is quantitative in nature and has distinct groupings with no overlap, e.g. the number of people in the class aged 6 or shoe size;
- *continuous* – data is on a continuous scale and is not divided into discrete or separate groupings, e.g. the heights of the children in the class.

The type of data collected will determine the most appropriate way of representing it. Categorical and discrete data can be represented as bar charts, pie charts or pictograms; continuous data is best represented as histograms, scatter graphs and line graphs.

Storage of data

Databases
These allow vast amounts of data to be stored in a structured way. The data can then be organised, sorted, retrieved and added to. Databases provide the opportunity for children to interact with data to explore meaning, relationships and patterns. The ease with which data can be presented in different graphical formats allows children to make decisions about the best way of presenting their data, sometimes illuminating new ways of looking at phenomena. Ready-prepared databases alleviate the burden of collecting information, allowing children to concentrate on the patterns and relationships in the data. Children can be encouraged to use databases to retrieve and interrogate data to answer particular questions, for example, 'do all blonde-haired people have blue eyes?' whilst designing and creating their own databases requires children not only to interrogate data but to have a deeper understanding of the value of the data stored. For example, if children are collecting information about minibeasts, they will have to decide which details are the most relevant to enter in order to provide adequate information about each organism. Data stored can be added to over time, so children can follow their own growth, for example, from the beginning to the end of the year. Data can also be added to year on year and so the effects of change over longer periods of time can be observed, such as the different types of plants growing in a designated 'wild area' in the school grounds.

Some of the advantages of using databases in primary science are that they:

- speed up the recording and reporting of the collected data;
- provide a simple mechanism for presenting the data so that children do not have to focus on graphing skills;
- provide a wide range of data;
- provide data stored over time, so comparison studies can be undertaken;
- allow children to spend time interpreting data;
- enhance knowledge and understanding;
- encourage skills of questioning, application of knowledge, prediction and hypothesising;
- develop curiosity, creativity and respect for evidence;
- assist in the improvement and accuracy of work.

The most common forms of databases found in primary schools are as follows:

- Branching tree or binary databases. These consist of data organised in a hierarchical manner. They allow the identification and sorting of objects, for example different types of materials, by posing and answering a set of sequential questions that have yes/no answers.

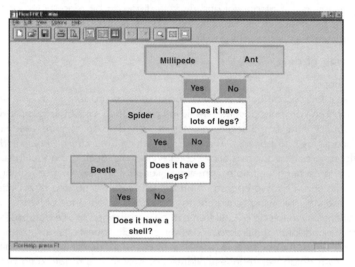

Branching tree or binary database

- Flatfile or tabular databases. A datafile contains information stored in records; within each record the information is organised into fields. This allows a particular record to be retrieved, for example, a particular tree and all the information about that tree is quickly and easily available. By interrogating the information from different records data can be retrieved from particular fields, for example, which trees in the datafile are deciduous?

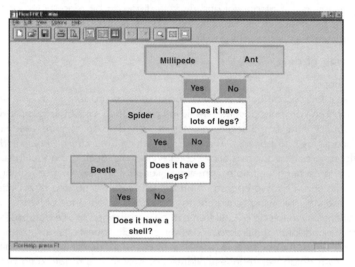

Flatfile or tabular database

- Relational databases are more complex than flatfile databases and allow children to access information through interrogation, making use of key words, indexes, menus and hyperlinks. Non-fiction CD-ROMs and World Wide Web search tools are the forms of this type of database most commonly found in primary schools.

Spreadsheets

These can be regarded as a special kind of database. Information, usually in the form of words or numbers, is entered onto a grid made up of cells, which are arranged in rows and columns. A number identifies each row and a letter each column, so each cell will have two identifying features e.g. A5, in the same way as coordinates on a map are used to identify a specific area. Spreadsheets allow data to be searched, sorted, re-arranged and presented graphically but, more importantly, formulae can be entered. This feature provides children with the opportunity to carry out rapid calculations and see the immediate effects of change on the data. Modelling different outcomes to a situation are possible and the 'what if?' questions can be asked and answered. Children may be investigating the strength of different types of yarn by adding masses to them; some scenarios are difficult and potentially dangerous to achieve in the classroom, but with the data available children could model the effects of much stronger yarns and greater masses.

Graphing programs

These allow children to create graphs easily and simply, taking away the tedium of manually creating them. The children can concentrate on the interpretation of the graph rather than become bogged down in its production. Graphing programs allow children to access and present data without having to understand the processes and procedures involved with databases and spreadsheets. However, you will have to know and teach the children the most suitable type of graphical representation for the data they are using.

A CLASSROOM SCENARIO FOR KEY STAGE 2 – A STUDY OF THE BIRD LIFE IN THE SCHOOL GROUNDS

You are planning work for your class of Year 3 or 4 children on *Life processes and living things*. You decide to undertake a study of the birds that visit different parts of our your school grounds, for example, the playground and a quiet garden area. You recognise that children will be gathering a variety of data about the birds as part of their work. This topic is a very good example of how generic software can be utilised in a real and meaningful context.

Teaching objectives

To teach children about the different bird life within the school grounds.
To use the features and functions of database software to develop scientific understanding.

Intended learning outcomes

To know that birds are living things and that they require food and water to survive.
To know that all birds have specific features in common.
To know that birds vary in their external characteristics and that species differ.
To know that these differences can be used for identification purposes.
To know that birds choose specific habitats that support their life processes.
To know that collecting and storing information in an organised way can help to find answers to questions.
To know that a database can be used to sort and classify information and to present findings graphically.

Links to QCA science scheme of work
4B: Habitats.

Areas of the National Curriculum for science at Key Stage 2 covered
Sc1: Scientific enquiry.
Sc2: Life processes and living things.

Links to QCA ICT scheme of work
3C: Introduction to databases.
4C: Branching databases.
4D: Collecting and presenting information: questionnaires and pie charts.

Areas of the National Curriculum for ICT at Key Stage 2 covered
Finding things out.
Developing ideas and making things happen.
Exchanging and sharing information.
Reviewing, modifying and evaluating work as it progresses.

Activities
The activities that the children could engage in using ICT include:

* using a branching database to familiarise themselves with the external features of common birds;
* observing the birds in the school garden and using the database to identify the birds;
* working in small groups, spending fifteen minute intervals over the period of one day collecting data about the number and variety of birds visiting the school garden and the playground. Additional data can be collected such as colour of feathers, size of the bird, male/female etc, depending upon age and attainment levels of the children in the class;
* entering data collected into a flatfile database (with the structure of the database having been designed for the purpose by the teacher);
* saving data;
* interrogating the data generated, asking questions such as 'What is the most common bird to visit our school grounds?' 'What is the rarest bird to visit our school grounds?' 'What colour is the most common? How many birds visit the school grounds in one day?' 'Is there a popular time of day for the birds to visit the school grounds?' 'Is there a difference between the number and type of birds in the playground and the garden?';
* producing their findings graphically in the form of bar charts and pie charts;
* considering their results and reporting to the rest of the class the answer to their particular question, providing an explanation of their findings;
* retaining the flatfile database of the birds which visit the school grounds for use by other children.

Additional activities
These activities could be alternatives to those suggested and used to provide some differentiation or used with a different year group. They act to extend the topic or provide additional work for those children who complete the original activities. Some ideas are:

* the data collection can extend over several days and the resulting information can, for instance be compared with the type of weather prevalent on particular days;
* the total number of birds and numbers of different types can be used to find the mean for each total across different days to enhance the validity of the data;
* an investigation about the food that birds eat can be undertaken. A variety of food sources, e.g. nuts, bread and seeds, can be introduced into the garden. Additional data can be gathered by monitoring the food which is eaten first, which birds choose which food source, whether providing additional food increases the number, and variety of birds visiting the garden;
* children will be able to collect data across the year or even over several years; thus a study of the bird population over time can be established;
* alternatives can be pursued by considering the effect of providing a more conducive environment for birds by improving the school grounds; for example, the provision of nesting boxes and bird tables for feeding, and planting introduced for cover and as a food source. The effects of altering the environment offer an area of suitable and interesting study.

Assessment

In this example you might want to assess whether the children can:

- recognise the significant features common to all bird species;
- identify different bird species correctly;
- provide suggestions about suitable data to be collected;
- use a database to organise and record data accurately;
- understand the significance of the data to be able to ask pertinent and relevant questions – for example about the variation between the birds, what the birds need in order to survive, the differences between one environment and another on the birds present;
- use the features of a database to answer their scientific questions.

DISCUSSION AND JUSTIFICATION FOR THE USE OF ICT

The topic described above will take several lessons to complete. The children will need time to be confident in their recognition of birds and in using a branching database. You will need to remind them about the structure of a branching database, perhaps by demonstrating one that you have already prepared. Whether you can demonstrate this to the whole class at one time or to separate groups depends upon the equipment you have in school. It may be useful to provide the children with several examples of branching databases to work through. You will also need to let them work through the branching database of familiar birds several times, and give them the time to familiarise themselves with the birds so that they will have the knowledge and confidence to recognise some of the birds when they start their observations.

The children will need to spend time observing the birds, and need to stay quiet and still if they are to collect worthwhile data. They should have the branching database easily accessible at this stage so that they refer to it during their observations and begin to recognise the birds that they see. A teaching assistant would be a very valuable asset during the data collection stages of this work.

The next session will involve small groups of children entering data on to a prepared flatfile database. Once all the data from the different groups are stored, children can choose specific questions they wish to ask and use the data to discover answers about the birds that visit the school grounds. Graphical representations will help them interpret the data and also provide printed material for display and presentation. Additionally, the information in the flatfile database can be retained, which would be especially useful if this were to become a long-term study and children were to return to the data each year.

Using ICT within this topic is based upon your knowledge and understanding that it is an efficient and effective means of recording and storing data that can be retrieved at a later date, added to or altered. The data can also be manipulated to provide answers to specific questions, and be presented in the form of pie charts and bar graphs easily, thereby taking away the time consuming and difficult task of creating these by hand. The graphs that are created allow the children to focus on interpreting them. In addition the children will gain valuable expertise in using, managing and creating databases of different types.

CONTINUITY AND PROGRESSION

The work described in the example for Key Stage 2 children will be grounded in work undertaken at Key Stage 1. Children at Key Stage 1 will have used ready-prepared branching databases and simple forms of graphical representation. In the context of *Life processes and living things* children may have collected data about themselves, for example eye colour and hair colour, and have some understanding of variation. They will also have been introduced to plants and animals in the environment, have collected data about them and know that different living organisms are found in different habitats.

Sensors and datalogging

Sensors monitor environmental conditions, for instances, temperature, light, sound, movement and humidity. *Datalogging* occurs when that data is collected and stored electronically for analysis and interpretation. Data-logging can take place remotely, for example, gathering data about the light intensity in different parts of the school grounds. The data is stored in a buffer box and later uploaded to a computer in the classroom and analysed. Alternatively datalogging can take place with the buffer box attached to the computer and the data is displayed simultaneously on the screen. The software used to display the information can be regarded as a special application of a graphing program. Datalogging equipment has many applications within science investigations.

Some of the advantages of using sensors and datalogging in primary science are:

- the speed and accuracy of measurements;
- the opportunity to take measurements over very short or very long periods of time;
- that measurements can be taken when it might be difficult or dangerous to take them in another way;
- that children can concentrate on interpretation of the graphical representations of the data produced;
- that a wide range of investigations are encouraged;
- that it facilitates repetition of investigations, thus encouraging development of the concept of experimental error as well as enabling the exploration of the impact of changing a wider range of variables;
- that it encourages children's analytical skills;
- that it helps to develop interest in physical and environmental phenomena;
- that it deepens scientific understanding of phenomena.

A CLASSROOM EXAMPLE AT KEY STAGE 2 – A SPONTANEOUS AND FORTUITOUS EVENT DURING WORK ON MATERIALS

It is often the case that suitable teaching situations occur after a topic has been covered, much to the annoyance of the teachers concerned! However, sometimes things do fall into place and the example described here is one of those occasions.

Your Year 4 class is studying materials and they come in from the playground very excited to find out more about the different types of gloves they are wearing. They want to know which gloves will keep their hands the warmest, as they were having a dispute about the relative effectiveness of each others' gloves at playtime. This provides you with an excellent situation in which to develop the children's knowledge and understanding of the thermal insulating properties of materials, develop their investigating skills and a splendid opportunity to use datalogging effectively within science.

You suggest that the children should bring in a variety of gloves and that they should plan an investigation to find out which glove is the most effective at keeping their hands warm. You tell them that they will be using datalogging equipment to record their findings and then introduce them to the equipment.

Teaching objectives
To teach children about the thermal insulating properties of different materials.
To investigate the insulating properties of different gloves in a practical way.
To teach children when it might be appropriate to use datalogging.

Intended learning outcomes
To know that different materials have different insulating properties.
To know that sensing devices can be used to monitor changes in environmental conditions.
To practise and develop skills; in particular:

- to plan an appropriate investigation;
- to record and report findings using datalogging equipment;
- to explain findings and evaluate the investigation;
- to work together in small groups and as a whole class team co-operatively.

Links to QCA science scheme of work
4C: Keeping warm.
5C: Gases around us.

Areas of the National Curriculum for science at Key Stage 2 covered
Sc1: Experimental and investigative science.
Sc3: Materials and their properties.
Sc4: Physical processes.

Links to QCA ICT scheme of work
5F: Monitoring environmental conditions and changes.

Areas of the National Curriculum for ICT at Key Stage 2 covered
Finding things out.
Developing ideas and making things happen.
Exchanging and sharing information.
Reviewing, modifying and evaluating work as it progresses.

Description of the investigation

Planning
The children may decide to use cups of hot water to take the place of warm hands with the cups being placed in the gloves. They will know that they have to make the investigation fair and the only variable has to be the different gloves. They must ensure that:

- the cups are the same size, shape, and made of the same material — paper cups from a vending machine are ideal;
- the temperature of the water at the beginning of the experiment is the same in all cups;
- the amount of water in each cup is the same;
- the sensors used to record the temperature in the different cups are of the same type;
- the sensors are immersed in the water to the same depth.

Predictions
It is likely that children will make a variety of predictions based upon prior knowledge, their visual and tactile observations of the gloves, for instance which is the thickest, fluffiest and so on. Their predictions may also be based upon a hypothesis, for example, that thick materials are the best insulators.

Carrying out the experiment
The children can work in small groups to set up the datalogging equipment with each group taking measurements for two or three gloves. The experiments will take several hours to complete and so children can set up their equipment and leave it whilst they continue with other work, and periodically observe the progress of the graph monitoring temperature loss.

Reporting and recording
At the end of a period of about four hours the children can share their findings with the other groups. All the children will be able to look at the different graphs as they are displayed on the screens. A whole class discussion can then take place to begin to discuss the findings. Each graph can be printed off to form a classroom display with the children providing a report of their particular investigation and relating it to the findings of all the other groups.

Explaining and evaluating
With all the graphs available to the children they will be able to make a reasoned judgement about the glove that is the best insulator and in addition to their knowledge of materials begin to provide some explanation of the results obtained.

They may also consider any improvements to their investigation, for example, two groups with the same gloves could be asked to check the reliability of the results. Additional investigations using the datalogging equipment may be considered; for instance, children could consider the insulating properties of materials to keep things cold by finding out if materials that keep things warm also help to keep things cold.

Assessment

In this example you might want to assess whether the children can:

- plan an appropriate investigation;
- use datalogging equipment correctly;
- record and report their investigation;
- provide a suitable explanation for their own findings and those of others.

DISCUSSION AND JUSTIFICATION FOR THE USE OF ICT

It may not be possible for you to accommodate all the children working at the same time on this activity due to resource or space constraints. You will have to decide, therefore, the best management of children and resources in your particular circumstances. However if you spread the activity out over too long a time period you will inevitably lose the spontaneity of the children's questions, which gave rise to the investigation in the first place.

The use of datalogging is ideal for this type of experiment for several reasons. Experiments like this always take several hours to complete and within the busy classroom it isn't always possible to take readings at regular time intervals. Some children may have difficulty in reading thermometers accurately and different children may take the readings throughout the duration of the experiment, thus adding to potential error. The datalogging equipment provides the children with the opportunity to concentrate on the analysis and interpretation of data from readily produced graphs rather than spend time on the process of collecting, recording and presenting data by themselves. In addition, there are certain obvious hazards to avoid when working manually with relatively hot liquids, unsupported cups and thermometers over a lengthy period of time. Additional benefits accrue from working as a whole class towards a common end such as learning to co-operate. In this example children have the opportunity to work as a team with each group's results important to the outcome for everyone. Using datalogging equipment assists the team effort because it removes some of the possible areas of experimental error that could occur if children were undertaking this investigation manually.

CONTINUITY AND PROGRESSION

Key Stage 1 children may not have used datalogging equipment although they may have had the opportunity to use sensors to detect the temperature in different parts of the classroom or used a temperature sensor to discover who has the warmest hands in the class for instance. They will however have investigated some effects of warming and cooling materials such as the factors involved in ice melting more quickly or slowly.

Electronic information sources

Information from electronic sources abounds; for example CD-ROMs, the Internet, intranets and data files. Children can make use of the information available to them to extend their science subject knowledge by researching specific topics or finding out answers to questions. There is a wealth of information that children can find out from electronic and multimedia sources in relation to science. These information-rich sources are ideal for extending children's knowledge and understanding of science. They can be used to tackle specific questions and allow children to make decisions about which information is required thereby enhancing and developing their research skills.

The speed with which children can access large volumes of information is advantageous and a class could access a wealth of information on a topic within one lesson which would take a great deal of time to research by other means. CD-ROMs often contain a vast amount of information on one particular topic or several related ones. It will be necessary for you to be able to evaluate a resource's suitability for the age of the children and the level of information it contains. In the same way you will need to steer the children to particular websites and pages within them so that they gain the most they can by directly accessing the information. You should also encourage children to evaluate the websites and CD-ROMs they access. A number of CD-ROMs and websites contain multimedia simulations and these have been discussed separately because of the particular links with science.

Some advantages of using electronic information sources are:

- the speed of obtaining information;
- the vast quantities of information available;
- the support provided for children with developing literacy skills, such as audio commentaries;
- deepening and extending subject knowledge;
- that curiosity is encouraged;
- that research skills are developed;
- that critical evaluation skills are developed.

A CLASSROOM SITUATION AT KEY STAGE 1 – PROVIDING ADDITIONAL SUPPORT FOR LESSONS ON ELECTRICITY BY EMPLOYING A CD-ROM MODEL

Your Year 2 class is spending several lessons exploring electricity. You are aware that the children need plenty of opportunities of first hand experience to investigate making circuits and exploring the requirements for a simple circuit to work. You consider that models of different circuits on CD-ROMs can enhance the children's learning by acting as a support to initial learning and as revision and consolidation. Additionally you can take advantage of the application by using it as an assessment opportunity.

Teaching objectives
To provide support through ICT for children's knowledge and understanding of simple electrical circuits.

Intended learning outcomes
To know what is required to make a simple electrical circuit work.
To understand how a switch works in a simple electrical circuit.
To be able to make a simple electrical circuit with different components using a CD-ROM simulation.
To be able to transfer and apply scientific knowledge and understanding.

Links to QCA science scheme of work
2F: Using electricity.

Areas of the National Curriculum for science at Key Stage 1 covered
Sc1: Scientific investigation.
Sc4: Electricity.

Links to QCA ICT scheme of work
1A: An introduction to modelling.

Areas of the National Curriculum for ICT at Key Stage 1 covered
Finding things out.
Developing ideas and making things happen.
Reviewing, modifying and evaluating work as it progresses.

Activities

The CD-ROMs should be available for children to access at all times through the lessons. You will probably need to demonstrate how to use the CD-ROM. The management of computer access will be determined by the number of computers and CD-ROMs you have. You can allow children to work at the computer independently, but there will be occasions when you will want to be with them, for instance to let them show you how they are making a particular circuit followed by specific intervention by you to assist their learning.

You can make use of the CD-ROM to:

- help children discover what they may have done incorrectly if they cannot get their bulb to light;
- revise what children have done with the practical equipment and consolidate their learning;
- allow children to demonstrate how to make a complete circuit;
- help children make more complicated circuits.

Assessment

In this example you might want to assess whether the children can:

- make a simple circuit;
- add a switch to the circuit and explain how it works;
- use a CD-ROM simulation to demonstrate their understanding of simple circuits ;
- understand that the CD-ROM simulation replicates the effects of the concrete apparatus.

DISCUSSION AND JUSTIFICATION FOR THE USE OF ICT

You will need to think carefully about the way in which you provide the additional experience of the ICT models to the children. They may think that it is better to work with the computer rather than with the wires, bulbs and batteries and perceive it as a more prestigious activity, to the detriment of their involvement in a practical scientific investigation. If the children make up a circuit correctly on a computer the bulb will always light or the buzzer sound. Unfortunately this is not always the case with the actual equipment for all sorts of reasons, such as poor connections in crocodile clips, batteries that are worn out, broken bulbs and so on. This may put children off and make them prefer the computer model. This would not be what you want or indeed intend. Careful preparation of the equipment and monitoring of the work the children do prior to accessing the computer will be essential if you are to avoid these problems. However, because the model always works it is a rewarding and worthwhile addition to the children's experience.

Using CD-ROMs in this way allows children the opportunity to check and rectify mistakes they have made using equipment. They can go back to the real equipment with the increased confidence gained from using the model and try again. The model gives children a chance to consolidate knowledge and understanding as well as to transfer and apply it in an alternative scenario. When the children work with the CD-ROM model you will be able to monitor what they are doing very easily and use it as an additional point for assessment.

CONTINUITY AND PROGRESSION

At a later stage, children will be able to make use of resources that allow them to create alternative and more complex circuits on screen by building circuits for particular situations, for instance two rooms with lights and separate switches. Accessing information via CD-ROM or websites can provide useful opportunities to research information, for example about the different ways of producing electricity or aspects of safety with regard to high voltage electricity. There are many aspects of electricity that are too dangerous or difficult for children to explore in a practical manner; the use of interactive models and simulations will provide children with the opportunity to find out the answers to questions that would be impossible to obtain in any other way. Children will become increasingly independent in their use of electronic information sources throughout the primary phase.

Control technology

Control technology makes use of programmable instructions to send signals to switches, motors and pumps to make them work at particular times or in a particular order. Control technology is present in many aspects of everyday machinery, such as washing machines and video recorders, and children should be able to understand how things operate and work automatically. The use of programmable toys is a first introduction to this area of ICT. Control programs and control-based CD-ROMs encourage children to behave in a scientific manner by considering different solutions to a particular problem, exploring those options, evaluating them and deciding on the best solution. The use of control technology provides valuable opportunities to demonstrate the links between science concepts and their application.

Some advantages of using control technology are that it:

* encourages children to think logically;
* encourages problem-solving skills;
* encourages co-operation;
* provides a context for the application of scientific principles;
* develops scientific understanding;
* stimulates curiosity.

A CLASSROOM EXAMPLE AT KEY STAGE 1 – CONTROLLING A FLOOR ROBOT

Imagine that your Year 1 children have been exploring the similarities and differences between invertebrates and where they are found. You happen upon a conversation between a group of children, which goes like this;

Child A. 'OOH look at that one running about!' whilst pointing to an ant.
Child B. 'Yes, and this one (snail) slides doesn't it?'
Child A. 'Yes, I've seen that one before but this one (wood louse) just seems to wander about the place. I wonder why it does that?'

You reflect on this conversation and especially the question posed by the last comment. It seems an ideal time to study the differences in the way invertebrates move and to consider why locomotion is important for their survival. You decide to encourage the children to use floor robots and try to programme them to imitate the locomotion of different invertebrates, for example a woodlouse and a snail.

Teaching objectives
To know how different invertebrates move.
To understand some of the reasons why animals need to move around.
To know that control devices must be programmed.

Intended learning outcomes
To observe how different invertebrates move.
To use observations to programe a floor robot to move like a snail and a woodlouse.
To observe what habitats invertebrates prefer.
To understand why invertebrates prefer particular habitats.
To produce and refine a set of instructions to control the movement of the floor robot.
To work together cooperatively to solve a problem.
To share solutions with the rest of the class.

Links to QCA science Scheme of work
2B: Plants and animals in the local environment.

Areas of the National Curriculum for science at Key Stage 1 covered
Sc1: Scientific enquiry.
Sc2: Life processes and living things.

Links to the QCA ICT scheme of work
2D: Routes: controlling a floor turtle.

Areas of the National Curriculum for ICT at Key Stage 1 covered
Finding things out.
Developing ideas and making things happen.
Exchanging and sharing information.
Reviewing, modifying and evaluating work as it progresses.

Activities
The activities that children could be engaged in are:

- observing different invertebrates and verbally describing how they move;
- translating movement into programmable instructions;
- using the floor robot to imitate the movement of invertebrates;
- observing and recording places invertebrates are found;
- discussing why the invertebrates are found in particular places and that their movement is not as random as it first appears but a purposeful exploration of their environment to search out specific things for their survival;
- observing invertebrates in a choice chamber;
- programming the floor robot to help direct the 'invertebrate' to find food, shelter, water etc.

Assessment
In this example you might want to assess whether the children can:

- observe differences in locomotion between invertebrates;
- understand why animals need to move;
- develop a sequence of instructions to move a floor robot focusing on direction and distance.

DISCUSSION AND JUSTIFICATION FOR USE OF ICT

The use of a floor robot can be a valuable addition to the children's work to help them understand that animals will look for specific places that provide them with the right conditions for survival, for instance, food and shelter. The children will improve their observational skills about the different ways in which the minibeasts move because they will have to use their observations and translate these into commands for the floor robot.

You will need to provide a clear space in the classroom for this work. It is likely that children will have to undertake this work rota fashion rather than as a whole class activity due to space and equipment constraints. It may therefore be a suitable addition to one of a number of activities in a circus. The children should be involved in developing their own questions to be addressed so scientific skills as well as subject knowledge and understanding are integral to the activity. The use of a programmable toy for Key Stage 1 is an ideal introduction to control technology. It provides the children with a simple device, which they can easily programme. The effects of their programming are immediately obvious, providing instant feedback about the validity of their instructions. The children can work together to solve the problems of translating what they have observed in real life, in order to make the robot move like the various invertebrates and to think logically about how an invertebrate might most easily move to a habitat where food or shelter can be found. They will have opportunities whilst undertaking these activities to reinforce the work they have done previously in observing the movement of invertebrates and their habitats and conditions for survival. Using robots in this way enables children to have a better understanding of some of the scientific principles behind the reasons for locomotion and survival. It improves their skills of observation, problem solving and co-operation as well as promoting curiosity. The activity could also be an invaluable addition to your contingency plans should the day you decide to go out prove to be unsuitable!

CONTINUITY AND PROGRESSION

Children will use the control features of floor, tabletop and screen robots programming them with increasing complexity. At Key Stage 2 children will employ other forms of control technology in different scientific contexts, including controlling light bulbs, buzzers and small motors. Children exploring light intensity could control when a light will switch on and off. This could be set as part of a problem-solving exercise to make the most efficient security lights for the school.

Communications technology

This aspect of ICT can be regarded as a subdivision of electronic information sources but it is worth considering as a separate entity for the purpose of indicating how it can enhance learning in science. Communication is a vital component of any scientific activity and with the advent of electronic communications in the form of email and intranets children are able to communicate with a much wider audience. *Intranets* (internal school networks, or sometimes Local Education Authority networks) facilitate the local sharing and exchange of information, such as research on a particular science topic or results from an experiment. Such sharing and exchange can enable children to collaborate; similarly it can result in larger datasets for experiments that would otherwise be inaccessible, assisting in the development of concepts such as the importance of replication and the relevance of experimental error. Children can communicate via *email* with their peers in other schools and in other countries, for example to help develop an understanding of the process of day and night by linking up with children in Australia. Children can also email professional scientists and ask specific questions, be given current and accurate information and gain an insight into how scientific communities operate.

Other advantages of using communications technology are that:

- a wide range of material is easily available;
- the information required is obtained very quickly;
- it provides the opportunities to obtain live data;
- it encourages communication skills;
- it encourages collaboration.

Simulation and modelling

The use of simulations and models is an important aspect of science education and is recognised as a valuable means of elaborating a principle or idea that may otherwise be difficult, dangerous or impossible to experience in any other way. In science *modelling* occurs when a computer is used to represent a 'real life' or imaginary situation. A *simulation* occurs when a model is used to predict the likely outcome of a real life or imaginary situation by changing certain parameters or variables. Computer-based examples of models and simulations include CD-ROMs and adventure games. CD-ROMs provide opportunities to explore aspects of science that would be impossible to achieve in a practical or first-hand way in a classroom situation, for example how the internal organs of the human body work. *Adventure games* provide a fictional situation in which exploration is encouraged and decisions have to be made, for example providing suitable environments for woodland animals to survive.

Some of the advantages of using models and simulations are:

- they make it possible to explore difficult or dangerous situations;

- they make it possible to explore events that would be impossible otherwise;
- they encourage 'what if' questions and as a consequence develop exploration, hypothesising, decision making and evaluation;
- they consolidate and extend subject knowledge by allowing alternative situations to be easily available.

A CLASSROOM STORY AT KEY STAGE 2 – USING SIMULATION AND MODELLING AND COMMUNICATIONS TECHNOLOGY TO LEARN ABOUT THE EARTH AND BEYOND

Your Year 5 class is about to start a series of lessons on the Earth and beyond. You decide as part of the work to provide the children with a set of challenges, which will allow them to work independently. They are to research an aspect of the topic and present this to the whole class. ICT offers great opportunities for this sort of independent research work. ICT is also very useful in this particular topic because of the difficulty in undertaking much of the work in a practical manner and the impossibility of experiencing some of the phenomena at first hand. You, therefore, decide the best way forward is to make use of a variety of simulations and models as well as communications technology to provide different learning experiences. These include CD-ROMs, the World Wide Web and email facilities.

Teaching objectives
To research appropriate information about the Earth and beyond using a variety of sources including CD-ROM, email, and the World Wide Web.
To present the information in a suitable format.

Intended learning outcomes
To know and understand how day and night occur.
To know and understand how the seasons occur.
To know and understand the phases of the moon.
To know and understand the nature of our solar system.
To be able to research appropriate and suitable information from a variety of sources.
To be able to record and report that information appropriately for the audience.

Links to QCA science scheme of work
5E: Earth, Sun and Moon.

Areas of the National Curriculum for science at Key Stage 2 covered
Sc1: Scientific enquiry.
Sc4: Physical processes.

Links to QCA ICT scheme of work
5B: Analysing data and asking questions using complex searches.
5C: Evaluating information, checking accuracy, and questioning and plausibility.

Areas of the National Curriculum for ICT at Key Stage 2 covered
Finding things out.
Developing ideas and making things happen.
Exchanging and sharing information.
Reviewing, modifying and evaluating work as it progresses.

Activities
The work will involve the development of research and reporting skills as well as an improvement in subject knowledge. Working in small groups the children will have to co-operate with one another, make decisions about how they will organise their work as well as how they are going to present it.

The various challenges you set will depend upon the level of attainment of the children but could include:

- how does day and night occur?
- why do we have seasons?

- what happens to the moon during one month?
- why is the Sun so important to us?
- what can you find out about the planets?

The children will be able to access information from the various sources available. They can use email to contact children in Australia and Iceland, to find out what time of day it is, what the season is and how it differs from what they are experiencing. Many websites have web cams (web cameras) by which children can actually see current conditions in other parts of the world. Simulations on CD-ROMs will enable children to further their understanding of phenomena such as the phases of the Moon, planetary motion and the orbit of the Earth around the Sun. The children could use science-specific software and the World Wide Web to find out as much information as possible about their question. Children can use their intranet to post useful information or recommend sources that might be of relevance to other groups.

Additional activities

Interesting information and answers to questions that children pose can make use of databases that you or children have prepared.

The following are some possible suggestions.

- How far does the Earth travel around the Sun in one day, one week, one month?
- How long would it take to get to Mars travelling at different speeds?
- How fast would you have to travel if you were to visit the Moon and get back in time for tea?

Children could then present their work to their peers, utilising any of the methods described in the next example.

DISCUSSION AND JUSTIFICATION FOR USING ICT

Children will need to be introduced to the various forms of ICT sources at their disposal and you will need to help them to avoid wasting their time by indicating and directing the most appropriate sources of information for their particular task.

The tasks will need to be organised either according to levels of attainment, or you may choose to allow the children to work in mixed ability or friendship groups.

The time available for the research as well as the presentation of findings will need to be planned, and the possibility of ongoing access to computers throughout the project would be helpful. However, if access is available in a computer suite where you have a time-tabled slot each week you may consider negotiation with other classes to add to your regular time in the suite. A longer-term project could result from connecting up with a school, for instance in Australia, to communicate throughout the year about key issues such as the seasons, differences in temperature, length of day and night and so on.

ICT in this example offers alternatives to the usual physical models and textual illustrations, through simulations and models of events and phenomena that are otherwise impossible or difficult to observe. It provides the children with the opportunities to explore new and unusual ideas and therefore stimulates interest and curiosity. It facilitates the children to work independently of you and cooperatively with each other. It allows children to communicate and share their ideas with each other as well as with children in other parts of the world. Collaborating in this way gives children some notion of how a scientific community operates. Children presenting their work electronically would have an additional opportunity to make use of ICT.

CONTINUITY AND PROGRESSION

In Key Stage 1 children will have already worked with simple simulations and adventure games and understood that they represent real or fantasy situations. Later children will use more complex simulations to develop the skills of making predictions, applying knowledge and understanding and decision-making. Whilst it is not a requirement for children to learn about the Earth and beyond at Key Stage 1, they are likely to have studied aspects of the seasons and the observable effects associated with day and night as well as understanding that the Sun is a source of light.

Publishing and presentation software

Communicating information effectively is a key skill in science, and reporting findings in a specific manner is one of the subject's main conventions. Word processing, graphics, multimedia and electronic slide presentation software can make this aspect of children's science work easier as well as more dynamic and exciting.

Word processing and *graphics* software allow children to enter text and images, and amend them to refine content and presentation in the light of reflection and evaluation. Word processing can also assist children to develop a conventional method of preparing their scientific reports. Teachers may assist in this process by preparing electronic templates or writing frames. Scaffolding the process in this way will allow children to gain confidence in writing their reports until they are skilful enough to do it independently. *Scanners* and *digital cameras* are increasingly being used for the generation of electronic images. Digital cameras will be discussed in more detail in Chapter 4. Scanners enable digital images to be made of hand-drawn diagrams, existing photographs, leaves and everyday (flattish) objects such as scissors. Images from digital cameras and scanners as well as those from other sources, such as clip art, CD-ROM and websites (subject to copyright) can be manipulated (cropped, enlarged, etc) and integrated into a range of publishing and presentation software to enhance the reporting and recording of scientific understanding. *Electronic slide presentation* software can assist children to organise and structure their findings to facilitate reporting back to the class or to a wider audience. *Multimedia presentation* software, incorporating sound and sometimes video, provides another sophisticated and dynamic presentation tool.

The advantages of using publishing and presentation software are that it:

- increases opportunities for modifying and evaluating work;
- enables children to improve the presentation of their work;
- assists in structuring and presenting written reports in a conventional manner;
- provides alternative formats for the communication of information;
- increases creativity.

A CLASSROOM SITUATION FOR KEY STAGE 1 – MAKING A POSTER PRESENTATION FOR A CLASSROOM DISPLAY

The children in your Year 1 class have been studying aspects of materials and their properties and you decided that a large display on the classroom wall of their work would provide a suitable and meaningful method of reporting and recording the children's work. You recognise that aspects of ICT would support the children in generating, modifying and displaying their work, in particular bringing together text, drawings, digital photographs, etc. You plan for the children to use a word processing package to achieve this. As part of their work the children have been looking at the range of materials used in the school and with knowledge acquired earlier in the topic have provided explanations for the use of the materials in specific places in the school building.

Teaching objectives
To know that a variety of materials exist.
To know that different materials have different properties.

To know that the properties of the materials determines their use.
To know that ICT can assist in the presentation of science work.

Intended learning outcomes
To observe the variety of materials used in the school building.
To identify the use of these materials.
To relate the use of the materials with their properties.
To experiment with layouts, refining presentation for display.

Links to QCA science scheme of work
1C: sorting and using materials.
2A: grouping and changing materials.

Areas of the National Curriculum for science at Key Stage 1 covered
Sc1: Scientific enquiry.
Sc3: Materials and their properties.

Links to the QCA ICT scheme of work
1B: Using a word bank.
1D: Labelling and classifying.
2A: Writing stories — communicating information using text.

Areas of the National Curriculum for ICT at Key Stage 1 covered
Exchanging and sharing information.
Reviewing, modifying and evaluating work as it progresses.

Activities
The activities that the children could engage in using ICT are:

- using word banks and graphics programs to present their findings about the materials used in their school;
- using word banks and preformed sentences to identify uses and properties of materials used in the school;
- choosing prescanned images and digital photographs to add to their poster;
- using a photograph and a floor plan of the school to identify where the materials are used and label them correctly;
- exploring alternative layouts.

Assessment
In this example you might want to assess whether the children can:

- identify different materials used in the school building;
- recognise the main properties of each of the materials;
- understand that the uses of the materials are related to their properties;
- use a word processor to produce and refine text and images that communicate meaning.

DISCUSSION AND JUSTIFICATION FOR USING ICT

With this age group you will need to prepare in advance a number of resources that the children will be using when they come to prepare their posters. These will include producing word banks in a word processing program and simple sentences, for instance to describe the properties of named materials and provide sample explanations for their use, from which children can make appropriate selections. For example, 'Glass is hard, it is waterproof and transparent.' 'Glass is a good material to make windows because it is transparent.' You may wish to have a range of photographs and pictures already scanned into the computer so that children can make a choice of these to add to their written work. The photographs of the materials could also be made into an identification game to reinforce subject knowledge by allowing the children to name the materials and state their properties. Additionally you may wish to include a photograph of the whole school and a floor plan, which the children can access, to label with the materials they have identified. Using ICT the children can have several attempts at the pictures, word banks and sentences to consolidate their subject knowledge and reinforce what they have done in a first hand practical manner. This is also a useful assessment opportunity. The use of word processing software means that children can rearrange their poster with ease, and it allows photographs and images to be inserted into whole documents in a professional manner, helping children to produce high quality pieces of finished work. Children can also experiment with colour and size of font to provide variety and interest in their poster.

CONTINUITY AND PROGRESSION

Using software for presentation within any context in science allows children to further their ICT capability and at Key Stage 2 children can produce electronic slide presentations and multimedia presentations of their work. Progression in science subject knowledge and understanding is enhanced by the opportunities for altering and modifying work; children are more inclined to correct inaccuracies and re-read what they have written when they know they can edit their work with ease.

This chapter has indicated the range and potential that computers have in enhancing the teaching and learning of primary science. The classroom examples indicate good practice but they are no means exhaustive; the intention is to provide you with a springboard to begin to experiment using ICT for yourself within your own setting.

ACTIVITY 1

The examples above have provided you with a range of ideas for employing ICT in science across the primary phase and in different parts of the science programmes of study. Spend some time referring to the Standards for ICT in *Qualifying to Teach* and the exemplification in the accompanying handbook and note the statements that would be fulfilled if you were to plan, teach and assess this work in school.

ACTIVITY 2

Choose one of the examples from the Appendix, or one of your own, and complete a teaching plan for the work showing how where and why you would incorporate the use of ICT. It may be worth your while to consider a few specific key questions with respect to your planning.

- Are the teaching objectives met by using ICT?
- Does ICT enable the teaching objectives to be met more effectively?
- Is the choice of ICT the most suitable for the work planned?
- How will the classroom organisation enable the teaching objectives to be met efficiently?
- Will the use of ICT assist children with special educational needs?
- Is the children's ICT capability increased?
- Can you assess the children's knowledge and understanding of science from the ICT based activity?

4 Using ICT in primary science without computers

This chapter will explore forms of ICT that are not computer-based (or do not initially require a computer) that can be used to assist children's learning in science. Some devices, such as digital cameras, can be used in the absence of a computer, but in order to explore and exploit the different functions of this equipment to its best advantage linking it up to a computer is necessary. Most primary schools will have ICT equipment that does not involve the use of a computer. The more common ones are:

- video cameras;
- pre-recorded videos and television broadcasts;
- audio recorders;
- pre-recorded tapes and radio broadcasts;
- overhead projectors;
- photography equipment, including digital cameras;
- programmable toys;
- digital equipment, including digital microscopes.

The use of *scanners* and *programmable toys* has already been discussed, and some equipment such as *digital stopwatches*, *light*, *sound* and *humidity meters* have very specific functions making it unnecessary to discuss these in detail. Using this type of equipment constitutes the use of ICT within your science lessons and like all other forms of ICT you need to justify its use by planning it as a valuable part of the children's learning experience. Digital microscopes are a relatively recent resource and their use will be discussed together with a classroom example utilising digital cameras.

Video cameras, pre-recorded videos and television broadcasts

Information has been collected and stored in readiness for viewing in all of these examples making it possible to discuss these together. *Pre-recorded videos* have the advantage that they can be viewed at any convenient moment in a lesson rather than being tied to a television broadcast time. Most schools have a system of recording *television programmes* so that they can be used in the same way as the pre-recorded videos mentioned above. *Camcorders*, whether they are used by yourself or the children, are also an invaluable tool in science.

Video recordings and broadcasts help to:

- increase scientific skills – for example observation, prediction, recording, analysing information, considering evidence and making conclusions;
- consider and develop questions;
- improve subject knowledge;
- increase curiosity and interest;
- provide a record that can be easily revisited.

In addition, using camcorders can provide opportunities to:

• record work in a different manner;
• increase independence;
• retain ownership of the work;
• promote decision-making skills;
• model the working practice of scientific communities;
• support children with special educational needs.

Pre-recorded videos and television programmes often provide information about a particular science topic which the children may find difficult to access from other information sources, for example, the underwater movement of animals. They may also contain images and special effects that would be more difficult to see in another way or even impossible to visualise, for example, time lapse photography of the growth of plants and moving images of spacemen on the Moon. Still photographs of these examples do not provide children with the same amount of information, the same level of interest or convey to the same extent the amazing phenomena that occur within the physical, chemical or biological world.

The use of camcorders is an aspect of ICT use that has great advantages in teaching and learning science. It can provide an instantaneous record of any work being carried out, and if children are allowed to use the equipment it puts them in the position of deciding what is worthwhile recording and thus gives them greater ownership of their work and increases their independence as learners. Videos can save time; for example, children can make a video recording to collect their observations and evidence during an investigation rather than drawing or writing everything. If the children need to make their own written records later on, they can use the video recording. It is also a valuable record in its own right for children to access, to remind them of the evidence they collected and to provide them with the opportunity to revisit and consolidate their subject knowledge.

Having a permanent record of outdoor activities means that you can continue with the work even if you are unable to revisit the area, for instance if the work was done off-site or if the weather is bad when you want to go out again. Returning to the example of the study of birds provided in Chapter 3, a video recording of birds visiting the school grounds would be a useful addition to help the children recognise and identify the birds prior to them making their survey. The whole class would be able to watch at the same time; a further advantage of a recording is that it can be run repeatedly for the whole class or for small groups, so that children do not have to spend a long time waiting to sight a bird. Similarly, the tape can be paused, rewound, stopped and started to facilitate teaching and discussion. The video can also form a permanent record of a particular point in the year and be used in subsequent years to make comparisons of the bird population at different points in the year and from one year to the next.

Video recordings can be used to assist young children or children with special needs where there is difficulty in making a written record of their work, and of course they can be used with equal success whether you are in or out of the classroom.

Camcorders can also be of use in school to record children's work, especially if they are doing a presentation. You will be able to use this as an opportunity to assess the children by viewing the recording later. Children can also develop their presentation skills by watching and analysing their own performances.

Whilst the use of video recordings can clearly be a very useful addition to your range of teaching tools there are some pitfalls that can reduce the value of this form of ICT. If video material is not used wisely children can see it as an easy option. They may not concentrate on what they are watching and consider it as a chance to 'switch off'. You will need to provide careful explanations of what and why they are going to watch, questions about what they have watched and a list of things to note whilst watching the video can also be useful ploys to ensure concentration. It is important that the material is suitably pitched for the age group you are teaching. There is also a danger in showing a whole video or television programme rather than editing it to only show the pertinent excerpts which can lead to loss of focus and an inefficient use of time.

Like any piece of equipment that is used for the first time, children will become excited about using a camcorder. It is worth considering very carefully how you will introduce what you want the children to do so that they can draw the most out the experience especially if they are recording themselves. You may have children who become very camera shy or perhaps just the reverse! (See Chapter 5 and the professional use of ICT for more details.)

A CLASSROOM EXAMPLE FOR KEY STAGE 2 – RECORDING THE PHASES OF THE MOON

The children in your Year 5 class are working on a topic covering aspects of the Earth and beyond. You have used a variety of resources including CD-ROM simulations to help them understand particular ideas; however, some children have found the phases of the moon a particularly difficult idea to grasp. You decide to spend some more time covering this and plan to use a camcorder to capture the Moon's orbit over the next 28 days.

Teaching objectives
To know that the Moon orbits the earth approximately every 28 days and its appearance from the Earth changes as a result.

Intended learning outcomes
To record the phases of the Moon in a variety of ways.
To understand that the appearance of the Moon changes in a regular cycle.
To know that this cycle takes place approximately every 28 days.
To understand that the change in appearance is due to the part of the Moon that we can see and is a result of the Moon orbiting the Earth.
To make predictions about the way the Moon's appearance changes.
To explain observations.
To be able to change ideas in the light of evidence presented.
To work with others co-operatively.
To program, record and review video using a video camera.

Links to QCA science scheme of work
5E: Earth, Sun and Moon.

Areas of the National Curriculum for science at Key Stage 2 covered
Sc1: Scientific enquiry.
Sc4: Physical processes.

Areas of the National Curriculum for ICT at Key Stage 2 covered
Finding things out.
Exchanging and sharing information.
Reviewing, modifying and evaluating work as it progresses.

Activities

Each morning the children will view the video of the Moon taken the previous evening. They will be asked to predict what they think the Moon will look like on the video and will be able to use their own observations from their Moon diaries to help. At the end of a week the children can edit the video to speed up the changes to the Moon so that by the time 28 days have passed they should be able to observe the complete cycle of the Moon's orbit.

Children will be responsible for setting the video camera at the correct time and so they will need to have some information, such as the weather report to know if the evening is going to be cloudy, clear up later etc; they will need to make judgements about the best time to set the recording each evening. This will involve further research and collaboration to try to ensure they get the best result, in this way they are very much modelling how a group of scientists would work on a project, thus increasing their skills of communication, research, deduction and decision making.

The children will be able to have discussions about the nature of the changes observed at different points in the cycle and consider why the Moon appears to look different at different points in the cycle. They should have access to the video recording during their science lessons and at other designated times to help them in their discussions. In addition to Moon diaries children could also have digital camera images of the Moon in different phases to download, print and use as an additional form of information. The video recording, digital images, models and children's drawings can form an interactive display together with CD-ROMs and information books to help children develop their understanding.

Assessment

In this example you might want to assess whether the children can:

* record information appropriately;
* make informed judgements on the basis of recorded evidence;
* know that the Moon orbits the earth every 28 days;
* understand that the change in appearance of the Moon is due to its orbit;
* work together to produce an interactive display.

DISCUSSION AND JUSTIFICATION FOR THE USE OF ICT

This work will take place alongside other aspects of The Earth and beyond; it is important to do this because the nature of the work will by necessity last at least 28 days. The children therefore need other activities to maintain their motivation and interest in the topic.

The use of the video camera in this example allows the children to observe the phenomena of the Moon's cycle at the time it is happening; they will be able to date the recording and know that what they can see on the video responds exactly to their own diaries. The children can also use the video as a permanent resource; it provides them with a joint resource for discussion and will help them develop a deeper understanding of what happens as the Moon orbits the Earth. Additional activities could include physical models and demonstrations.

The use of ICT in this example shows that it can act as an invaluable additional resource providing information in a different format, ensuring that evidence is captured. The evidence is not transitory or ephemeral in the same way as observing the Moon each evening; it also means that the evidence can be collected when the Moon is more likely to be more visible, for example, later in the night when children would be asleep. It will help to maintain interest in the collection of data because keeping a diary for 28 days can be difficult for some children. The equipment is portable so that the teacher can take it home at the weekend and video on evenings when no one would be in school.

A video or CD-ROM of the Moon's orbit could be equally good; however, being able to capture the information in real time will add to children's understanding. The children's own video could be supplemented by having these professionally-made resources available.

Doing the work in this way will promote children's interest, enthusiasm, motivation and subject knowledge, and it will help them work together co-operatively on a project. They could present their work to the whole school. If time permits, a joint project with another school in a different part of the world could be set up so that the children could exchange information via email.

CONTINUITY AND PROGRESSION

During Key Stage 1 children will have spent time working together on different types of science topic and will have some experience of developing their scientific skills. They should be able to practise and improve the skills required within this project. The children will have worked on topics such as light, and know that the Sun is a primary source of light and that the Moon is a secondary source. Early in Key Stage 2 children will have looked in more detail at the Earth's orbit of the Sun, studying phenomena like night and day and changing seasons. They may also have had some opportunity to study the planets.

Children can become more confident in a different form of technology and understand that computers are not the only form of ICT that they can use to help them learn.

Audio recorders, pre-recorded tapes and radio broadcasts

Using pre-recorded audio material provides children with another learning format. *Audio tapes* can be used at an appropriate moment within a topic or lesson, or be made available for children to access as a learning resource for themselves. Similarly, they can form an additional element on a science interest table. They can provide additional information that may be used to help children research their science work. Recordings might be, for example, the story of a famous scientist and their work or explanations of science investigations which children have previously undertaken.

Using blank audiocassettes to record children's work enables children to concentrate upon the science without the worry of physically recording their work. This may mean that they have the opportunity to develop their scientific thinking and subject knowledge as well as develop their scientific understanding to a much greater extent rather than spend time writing up a report. It may also mean that children's oral and listening skills are enhanced. All children may benefit from the use of audio recording at times during their science lessons, but you may find it particularly advantageous for assessing very young children or children with special needs.

Some advantages of using audio material in science are:

- to provide an additional and alternative learning format;
- to encourage children to research information and ideas;
- to record information;
- to aid assessment;
- to promote peer learning;

- to develop specific scientific skills;
- to increase subject knowledge;
- to develop oral and listening skills.

One of the advantages of using audio to record children's work, whether carried out by the children, teacher or teaching assistant, is that it can be much less intrusive and easier to manage than using a video recorder. Children may be less conscious of the ICT being used and therefore work more naturally, which will provide a truer picture of their level of attainment.

Audio material has to be appropriately pitched to the level of attainment of the children and clear guidance needs to be provided in order to make the best use of the recording in the same way as video material. This can be especially important if children are independently listening to tapes using headphones!

A CLASSROOM EXAMPLE AT KEY STAGE 1 – USING AN AUDIOCASSETTE TO INTRODUCE CHILDREN TO A RANGE OF DIFFERENT SOUNDS

Your Year 1 class is studying sound and as part of their work you want them to appreciate and understand that sounds can be very varied and come from a variety of sources. You decide to make use of pre-recorded audio tapes and recordings made by the children as a way of helping them achieve the learning outcomes.

Teaching objectives
To understand that sounds come from a variety of sources and that they differ.

Intended learning outcomes
To know that there are different types of sound.
To identify common everyday sounds.
To be able to recognise the source of everyday sounds.
To develop observational skills.
To begin to recognise particular features of sounds such as pitch and volume.

Links to QCA science scheme of work
1F: Sound and hearing.

Areas of the National Curriculum for science at Key Stage 1 covered
Sc1: Scientific enquiry.
Sc4: Physical processes.

Links to QCA ICT scheme of work
1C: The information around us.

Areas of the National Curriculum for ICT at Key Stage 1 covered
Finding things out.
Developing Ideas and making things happen.
Exchanging and sharing information.
Reviewing, modifying and evaluating work as it progresses.

Activities
You have decided to provide the children with a pre-recorded tape of some everyday sounds and you introduce this as a guessing game for the whole class. This activity will provide an interesting way of starting the topic and give children an opportunity to develop their skill of observation. They will be asked to identify the sounds and share their findings with the whole class, they will be asked to say what they thought the sounds were and provide reasons. The tape will be available for the children as a resource to access during the remainder of the time spent on this topic. Children will then go on a sound

walk to help them identify more sounds in their environment. Following this activity the children will be work in small groups with an adult and make a audio tape of five sounds that they would like to record as a challenge for the rest of the class. These tapes will be available for everyone to listen to and think about what sounds children have recorded. The children should try to identify the sounds and provide a reason for their answers.

These activities will assist children in:

* developing their skills of observation and understanding that observation can mean using senses other then sight;
* reasoning to be able to say what a sound is and why;
* planning an activity based on prior observations;
* peer teaching;
* deepening their understanding of the variety of sounds and their sources;
* developing understanding that sound travels from a source and what happens as it travels further from the source;
* beginning to develop some ideas about pitch and volume.

Assessment
In this example you might want to assess whether the children can:

* identify common sounds and where appropriate their source;
* provide reasons for their decision;
* work together co-operatively;
* explain how sound changes as it moves from its source;
* begin to suggest ideas about volume and pitch.

DISCUSSION AND JUSTIFICATION FOR THE USE OF ICT

The initial activity will provide children with an immediate interest in the topic; it will stimulate discussion, curiosity and enhance their skill of observation. They will be asked to provide reasons for their answers; in doing so the children will have to consider the evidence they have, compare different sources of evidence and evaluate them in order to provide a rational answer. They will then have to use the information they gather from their sound walk to plan what they are going to record. At this point it may be possible to differentiate the tasks by introducing the ideas of volume and pitch and distance from the sound source.

The use of audio material allows you to have a record of the children's work, gives them an opportunity to learn using a different format and enables the children to learn to use each other's ideas. Making use of ICT allows the learning outcomes to be achieved much more easily and in a worthwhile manner. It provides children with the experience of another form of ICT and enables them to become more proficient in its use and application.

CONTINUITY AND PROGRESSION

The work completed at Key Stage 1 will form the basis for children in Key Stage 2 to use audio recordings linked to a sound sensor to undertake investigations such as volume of a sound received in relation to the distance from its source or sound insulation. Investigations like these will develop and enhance skills such as prediction, hypothesising, planning and evaluating. The opportunity to move from a qualitative to a quantitative investigation also allows the children to progress.

Overhead projectors

Overhead projectors are one of the most under-used ICT resources in school. They can be used very effectively in the classroom to assist children's knowledge and understanding of a variety of scientific topics by being used conventionally to present information. They can also be used in a number of imaginative ways, to provide worthwhile and valuable teaching and learning resources. Transparencies can be made to produce life size versions of biological diagrams and drawings by projecting the image onto a wall rather than the screen. Hinged or sliding overlay transparencies to build up a picture of complex systems such as the inside of a human body, the structure of a flowering plant, the solar system or the rain cycle are also useful teaching resources. In addition, hinged acetates can be used to good effect, for example, to build up a complete electric circuit or the life cycle of a frog. Some can be bought commercially but you can make these yourself, or when appropriate allow children to make and use them. Producing acetates yourself is not only cheaper but they can be very specific both in terms of the content and age range being taught.

Allowing children to make acetates gives them the opportunity to present what they have done in a different format, gives them increased confidence in presenting their ideas, providing an opportunity to articulate their ideas which in turn helps to increase understanding and also gives you an assessment opportunity!

Using the bulb as a source of light can also produce some excellent results, such as simple shadow formation and the production of a 'rogues gallery' of the silhouettes of the children in the class. It can also be used as the 'Sun', for instance, when modelling day and night or the phases of the Moon, as well as investigating shadow formation and the factors affecting the nature of shadows. At Key Stage 2 these activities can be developed into a quantitative investigation by exploring the distance between the shadow, the object and the source of light.

Children can present their work to the rest of the class using the overhead projector and this means that the children presenting the work can read what they have written and the others in the class can also easily see the work. Gone is the trial of holding the work up to the rest of the class and struggling to read it at the same time! It also provides you with another assessment opportunity. Handwritten or computer-generated text and/or images can quickly and easily be enlarged and photocopied onto acetates.

Using overhead projectors in science can:

- promote interest;
- increase scientific understanding and subject knowledge;
- offer alternative ways of investigating particular phenomena;
- develop independence and ownership of work;
- provide alternative formats for recording work;
- provide opportunities to present work;
- promote confidence and oral skills;
- offer assessment opportunities.

A CLASSROOM EXAMPLE AT KEY STAGE 2 – INVESTIGATING THE STRUCTURE OF THE HUMAN AND OTHER VERTEBRATE SKELETONS

The children in your Year 4 class are about to start some work on the locomotion of animals, in particular humans and other vertebrates. You do not have access to real or model skeletons but you want the children to appreciate the size of the bones in the human skeleton, compare them with other animals and work interactively with the materials at your disposal. You decide to make overhead transparencies of the skeletons you will be studying and project them in such a way to provide a life size images.

Teaching objectives
To know the structure and function of vertebrate skeletons.
To compare different vertebrate skeletons and understand why they have become adapted.

Intended learning outcomes
To explain the functions of the human skeleton.
To name the main bones of the skeleton.
To explain how different bones are adapted for different functions.
To describe and explain how the skeletons of different vertebrates are adapted.
To prepare a set of acetates to present to the class on a researched aspect of the skeleton.

Links to QCA science scheme of work
4A: Moving and growing.

Areas of the National Curriculum for science at Key Stage 2 covered
Sc1: Scientific enquiry.
Sc2: Life processes and living things.

Areas of the National Curriculum for ICT at Key Stage 2 covered
Finding things out.
Developing ideas and making things happen.
Exchanging and sharing information.
Reviewing, modifying and evaluating work as it progresses.

Activities
A range of activites is possible using an overhead projector.

- Use the overhead projector to study the human skeleton and label the main bones. This activity can be used with the whole class or small groups, and the labels can be added in a variety of ways; for example, they can be ready prepared and placed in the correct position on the overhead projector, the image can be projected on to large sheets of paper and children can write on the paper or the labels can be prepared on card and positioned on the wall using Blutac.
- Use the projected image to compare different bones, for example, size, shape and position, and consider their functions.
- Make a transparency to show how different bones e.g. femur and pelvis, or humerus, radius and ulna are articulated.
- Compare and contrast the skeletons of different vertebrates, e.g. fish, bird and rabbit. The overall size of the skeletons as well as the size and structure of homologous bones are possible avenues for study to enable children to consider how the skeleton has become adapted for its environment.
- Research an aspect of skeletal function or adaptation and present this as an overhead transparency presentation to the rest of the class.

These activities will help children to:

- improve their subject knowledge and understanding;
- develop research skills;
- promote interest and curiosity;
- develop their presentation skills both orally and visually;
- promote communication skills.

Assessment
In this example you might want to assess whether the children can:

- describe the main functions of the skeleton;
- label the bones of the human skeleton;
- understand the way certain bones have become adapted for particular functions;
- understand why skeletons of different animals have become adapted;
- articulate their ideas and present information to the whole class in an interesting and stimulating manner using ICT.

DISCUSSION AND JUSTIFICATION FOR THE USE OF ICT

Life-size enlargements of resources like a skeleton, which primary schools do not usually have, is clearly a useful and interesting application of the overhead projector. It provides the children with a much more realistic visualisation compared to a small diagram in a book. It means that the whole class can be taught if you wish to do so, or groups of children can use it throughout the sequence of lessons. The acetate is a cheap resource if made 'in house' and so a large number can be produced quickly and cheaply. Games or assessments are possible by having labels for the bones and their functions and asking children to sort them out. Comparing the different skeletons can be achieved by having several overhead projectors in the room and projecting each image to the correct size, children will be able to make comparisons such as size of the whole skeleton, size and structure of homologous bones, and appreciate how each animal's skeleton has become adapted. Interest is maintained by enabling children to research different aspects and to engage in peer learning through their presentations. Scientific skills such as communicating findings, considering evidence and observation as well as knowledge and understanding will be enhanced.

CONTINUITY AND PROGRESSION

The overhead projector can be used to provide a life size body outline at Key Stage 1 for children to name the main external parts; they can also have outlines of other animals to compare, and a simple version of the human skeleton could also be used. For children at Key Stage 2 additional resources can be provided such as overlays of the internal organs of the body, or the addition of muscle to the skeleton.

Photography equipment

Still photographs can be a useful additional resource in science lessons; these can be already produced or the children can use a camera to generate their own. Photographs can enable children to view aspects of science that they might not otherwise have access to, or that would be unsafe to have first hand experience of, for instance wild animals, dangerous situations or unusual habitats. They can help children broaden their experience by providing a wider context in which scientific principles are exemplified and as a consequence help to stimulate curiosity and engender a questioning attitude and increase observational skills.

When children are allowed to take their own photographs they can use these as a form of recording, making the task of writing or drawing less arduous although this should not always be avoided! When children use the camera themselves they have to decide what they will photograph which can lead to a greater sense of ownership of the work. It puts the children in control of their own learning and assists independence. The use of a camera can assist in reporting an investigation by having photographs available of the different stages of the experiment. Children can return to what they did using the photographs as prompts; in this way there is a greater chance of accuracy as well as the opportunity of more detailed discussions thereby promoting better subject knowledge.

Photographs can be used to record the germination of seeds and the subsequent growth of the plants, especially if they are used in conjunction with original drawings and measurements. They can be useful to record changes to the environment throughout the year, for instance observing the changes to trees or to a specific tree from September to July. A very interesting and meaningful display is then possible. Photographs from a polaroid or digital camera have an immediacy that is lacking in conventional photography and therefore can be more useful for recording purposes in the classroom.

Digital cameras focus and take images in a similar manner to conventional cameras. The difference comes in the storage of those images. Digital cameras have no film; instead the image is held as digital information in the camera's memory. Most cameras are supplied with software that enables images to be downloaded onto a computer, manipulated if required and saved. The images can be easily incorporated into other documents by children and can also be emailed to children in other schools as part of a joint project, for instance on different types of habitats in different parts of the world. Selections can be enlarged helping children to observe greater detail and therefore stimulate curiosity as well as increasing subject specific knowledge.

If the quality of digital photographs does not provide sufficient detail, a *digital microscope* is a very useful addition, providing a means for children to observe fine detail easily. Digital microscopes display enlargements at between ten and 200 times directly onto a computer screen. This ensures that a group or class can all see the image at once. Both still and moving images can be captured, illustrating the structure of fabric or the movements of an ant for instance. A time-lapse option allows the capture of stages of growth or decay over time.

Some advantages of using photographs are:

- enhancing curiosity;
- developing subject knowledge;
- enhancing observational skills;
- promoting questions;
- forming a permanent record;
- providing a simple way of recording to allow children to focus on the science.

A CLASSROOM EXAMPLE AT KEY STAGE 1 – A STUDY OF THE COMMON INVERTEBRATES AND THEIR HABITATS IN THE SCHOOL GROUNDS

You are studying the plants and animals in the local environment with your Year 2 class. Your focus is the variety of invertebrates found in different parts of the school grounds. You decide that digital cameras will help with recording, especially as you do not intend to spend a long time outside involving the children in observational drawings as you have already done this in class using snails. You also want to produce a multimedia record of the common invertebrates found and their habitats to assist in the further development children's knowledge and understanding together with their skills of prediction and evaluating evidence.

Teaching objectives
To know that there are a variety of invertebrates living in the school grounds and that these animals can be found in different habitats.
To understand why the invertebrates are found in different habitats.

Intended learning outcomes
To know that there are a variety of invertebrates living in the school grounds.
To predict where different animals might be found.
To make a photographic record of the animals and the places they are found.
To use evidence from records and display to explain why different invertebrates prefer different habitats.

Links to QCA science scheme of work
2B: Plants and animals in the local environment.

Areas of the National Curriculum for science at Key Stage 1 covered
Sc1: Scientific enquiry.
Sc2: Life processes and living things.

Links to the QCA ICT scheme of work
1C: The information around us.
1D: Labelling and classifying.

Areas of the National Curriculum for ICT at Key Stage 1 covered
Finding things out.
Developing ideas and making things happen.
Exchanging and sharing information.
Reviewing, modifying and evaluating work as it progresses.

Activities
Small groups of children can be taken outside to identify two contrasting habitats and photograph them and the invertebrates they find in each. The children should predict what invertebrates they think they might find and then explore their chosen habitats. The children should spend some time considering whether their predictions were correct or not and begin to provide some reasons for their answers. Some simple form of identification key could be useful for the children to have access to at this stage.

In the classroom the children will use their photographs to compare and contrast the two habitats and the invertebrates found in each one. Using the photographs to identify external features of the invertebrates will help children develop their ideas about why particular invertebrates are found in certain habitats, and by referring to their original predictions they will be able to evaluate the evidence to see if they are supported or not. A digital microscope could enhance this aspect of the work especially if the photographs do not show fine detail when enlarged. The photographs and the children's ideas can be made into a poster to share with the rest of the class.

As a whole class the children will share the information gathered from different groups and this will provide opportunities to underpin their own findings.

An interactive multimedia presentation, incorporating some of the digital images, as well as other aspects of the children's work will help the children consolidate their ideas about variation and adaptation as well as allowing them to practise their skills of prediction.

Assessment
In this example you might want to assess whether the children can:

* recognise the common invertebrates found in the school grounds;
* identify different habitats and the particular physical conditions found in each;
* be able to predict where different animals might be found;
* relate the animals found to the physical conditions of different habitats;
* use recorded evidence to recognise the relationship between invertebrates and their habitats;
* begin to understand that animals are adapted to survive in particular environments.

DISCUSSION AND JUSTIFICATION FOR THE USE OF ICT

The use of digital cameras to help children record animals as well as their habitats is a useful strategy to save time, provide a permanent record and allow the children to use the images in their work. Manipulating the images they produce by enlarging will enhance children's observational skills and stimulate further questions and curiosity about the animals. Having the photographs allows the children to continue their work even if the weather becomes unsuitable in subsequent lessons, as they have no need to go back outside. As a class much more information will have been produced in a short space of time than could have been achieved if the children had recorded their findings by drawing and describing the invertebrates and their habitats. The children therefore have access to a greater range of data and an opportunity to share each others' work.

Digital photographs will enable you to produce an attractive and accurate multimedia presentation that the children can use to practise their skills of prediction whilst furthering their understanding of invertebrates and their habitats. You can also store some of the images and begin to develop a data bank of what invertebrates can be found in the school grounds. This can be added to in subsequent years and form the basis of comparison study over time.

CONTINUITY AND PROGRESSION

Children in Key Stage 1 may already have some experience of the different types of habitats to be found in the school grounds. They may have looked at different animals and have some prior learning about their external features as described in Chapter 3. The work in this example builds on previous experience by advancing the children's knowledge and understanding of the variety of animals to be found, relating them to particular habitats, recognising that different invertebrates have specific requirements and that particular features allow them to survive in these environments. Children's prediction and observational skills will be developed and enhanced by considering the habitats and the invertebrates found there. They will also compare their predictions with the recorded evidence and provide explanations for their answers.

In Key Stage 2 children will develop their knowledge and understanding of this aspect of science by undertaking further work on habitats, biodiversity, adaptation, life cycles, food chains and interdependence. Children will further develop their use of digital and conventional photography as a recording mechanism, becoming more independent.

Primary science has for some time made use of some applications of non-computer technology. This chapter has sought to remind us of how these applications as well as the newer technologies, e.g. digital cameras, can be used to improve and enhance the teaching and learning of primary science.

ACTIVITY

Prepare a sequence of lessons for a science topic that you are about to teach and plan for the use of as many non-computer based ICT teaching and learning opportunities as you can. Develop a rationale for their use and show how their use assists children's science and ICT knowledge, skills and attitudes.

5   Managing ICT in primary science

The management of ICT within the context of primary science operates at a variety of levels and involves different people in the process.

These can be considered as:

- professional level – the individual teacher managing ICT;
- classroom level – managing ICT within the classroom setting;
- whole-school level – the role of the science and ICT subject managers.

Professional use of ICT

A range of ways in which you can utilise the features of ICT to effect are briefly explored below. These examples are neither comprehensive nor confined to primary science in their application. You may find some of the ideas immediately and directly relevant; there may be applications which you will think about for the future. Equally you will be prompted to think of other uses, which are not mentioned here, but which will be similarly efficient and effective.

Planning, preparing and resourcing
With a little investment of time, word-processing software can greatly increase efficiency in preparation and customisation.

Planning
Plans held in electronic format are easier to amend in the light of experience, acquisition of new resources or a particularly short half-term. Relevant sections can be copied and pasted from the scheme of work to medium term, weekly and lesson plans.

Resourcing
ICT can be useful in the generation of both paper-based and electronic resources to support teaching and learning activities. Paper-based resources include writing frames, work sheets, cloze procedures and help sheets. Electronic resources also include writing frames as well as sentence and word banks of a generic nature or to support individual activities or children, and text deletion activities.

Display
Banners and labels can be quickly and easily printed at varying sizes making effective use of presentational tools.

The World Wide Web provides access to a range of resources, which can assist you in the preparation and planning of primary science.

Subject knowledge
There is a wide range of web pages that you may find helpful for revising and updating science subject knowledge when preparing and planning for teaching. You must remember to exercise caution and, if necessary, check

facts with other sources as many web sites are not subject to rigorous editing and checking processes.

Teaching ideas
Increasingly there are exemplars available on web sites designed to assist teachers planning to integrate ICT into primary science. These show worked ideas, often offering planning, resources, classroom management advice and assessment notes which you can use or customise. See, for example BECTa at www.becta.org.uk/technology/index.html (then select ICT in the Curriculum, followed by science, primary focus and ICT Scheme of Work) at www.becta.org.uk/technology/index.html

Teaching resources
There are whole websites and portals (web pages which provide links to lots of other pages) dedicated to sharing teaching resources and activities online. These include Teaching Ideas (www.teachingideas.co.uk). On the Web you will find resources which you can save, print off and use in the classroom as well as links to the activities described below.

Teaching activities
A wide range of quizzes and other interactive activities are available online. The BBC produces some useful ones, see Digger and the Gang for science activities across the primary age phase.

Models
It can be useful, especially for trainees, to view children's science work on school web pages. Not only might this provide ideas for activities and links to resources, but it is helpful to see the range of children's attainment to assist with planning for differentiation.

Assessment, monitoring, recording and reporting
There are various aspects of ICT that can assist you in these professional activities.

Assessment
Word processing is helpful for the drawing up of assessment pro formas, both for teacher use and child self-assessment purposes. Video and occasionally audio recording may be useful – for instance, to observe the interactions of a group of children as they plan an investigation where traditional observation may not be an option due to the supervision of other groups and activities or the wish not to inhibit or affect the children's discussions.

Recording and monitoring
Many teachers prepare a spreadsheet at the start of the year listing each child's name with a series of empty columns. These are then put to a number of uses, one for maths, one for science, etc. Each activity or learning outcome is listed and a code (blank, outline circle, filled circle for instance) is used to record and monitor progress. Please remember that any such data held on children is subject to the requirements of the Data Protection Act 1998. As such it must be held securely and deleted when no longer required. Digital cameras and video can be used to record stages and outcomes of science activity which are difficult or impossible by other means.

Reporting
The publication of children's work on school websites not only provides a real audience and purpose for the work, but can provide another mechanism through which teachers can communicate with parents about children's achievements.

Communication and professional development

ICT, and in particular the Internet, provides a range of opportunities for teachers to communicate and exchange ideas and information with respect to their teaching of primary science. These as such constitute professional support and development.

Discussion fora and newsgroups
The NGfL, professional associations and other websites provide access to fora or electronic bulletin boards where teachers can ask questions and discuss professional issues. These may range from teaching ideas on ourselves and other animals to issues of pedagogy and professional ethics. A similar facility is provided via email called a newsgroup. This is essentially an email distribution list. Any member can ask a question or offer a comment and others will respond and debate the issue.

Professional associations
There are a number of relevant teachers' professional associations, for science and ICT. These include the Association for Science Education (ASE), Micros and Primary Education (MAPE) and the Association for ICT in Education (ACITT). They provide a range of resources, professional development opportunities such as conferences, communication opportunities and other support. Each has a website.

Classroom management of ICT

When you plan for the use of ICT in your science lessons, what you can achieve is clearly determined by the resources and facilities you have at your disposal. What can be completed in one lesson with the whole class in a computer suite may not be possible in a classroom with one or two PCs; however, more isn't always better and with careful organisation and management you can provide excellent opportunities in the classroom. You also need to think in the broadest possible terms and make use of other resources to their full advantage, as we have illustrated in previous chapters. Your decisions about how you intend to manage the class will also be determined by:

- the activity or activities;
- the age and level of independence of the children;
- the presence or absence of additional adult support;
- ensuring equality of access;
- health and safety.

Making use of ICT within different organisational lesson structures will give children the widest possible access to ICT, provide them with alternative learning formats, create interest and help you to achieve your teaching objectives. There are several ways of managing and organising science lessons and you will need to match the best organisational strategy to meet your teaching and learning objectives, whilst remembering those factors which may prescribe what you can do.

Whole-class teaching

Whole-class science teaching is useful to introduce a topic or lesson, to round up a lesson or as a demonstration. It avoids repetition by the teacher and can save time, it ensures all the children have be taught or shown the same material, for instance, a video about the dangers of electricity, and it allows the teacher to question the whole class and gauge levels of attainment. ICT applications that can be employed effectively include interactive whiteboards, overhead projectors, a computer linked to a large screen, video and audio recordings. This strategy requires minimal resources but can be limiting for children in gaining first-hand experience.

Small group teaching

Co-operation and collaboration are key advantages of small group work; discussions and children taking responsibility for particular tasks also feature highly. It is important when using ICT in these situations that you provide children with the opportunity for them all to participate; for example, a group of children using a floor robot should be given enough time for each child to programme it. Some of the possible group work arrangements are discussed.

- Each group is engaged in the same activity. This can be considered a version of whole class teaching and has the advantages of being relatively easy to monitor and tasks can be differentiated. The arrangement requires having a high level of resources and increasingly schools have computer suites that can accommodate a whole class. It may be useful to have children work on data collected from an investigation and to use generic software to prepare graphs, or to interrogate or add to a database after some fieldwork. However, it is unlikely that many primary schools have class sets of, for example, datalogging equipment, video recorders or floor robots and different groupings will have to be considered to maximise their use.

- Each group is doing different things, which means the level of resources required is relatively low and if additional adult support is available, an activity can take place outside the classroom, for example, using digital cameras to record the materials used in the school building. There are two main ways of organising this type of group work. The first involves different groups doing a different activity and sharing it with the rest of the class. It is relatively easy to monitor and is a useful strategy if one activity requires more adult supervision than the others. This type of organisational structure means that you can make one activity ICT based, for example, children could investigate the light intensity of different light sources using datalogging equipment whilst the rest of the class explored other aspects of light. However it will be important if you employ this strategy that the other groups are given the opportunity to use to the ICT application at a later date. The second involves a number of activities on which the children work in rotation, sometimes called a *circus of activities*. The circus of activities is not so easy to monitor and requires careful timing of each activity. An ICT based activity can be easily added to the circus but this must be achievable in the time available and therefore needs to be very focused, for example, completing specific electric circuits using a CD-ROM. Alternatively, using several different ICT applications at one time can make use of limited resources, for example, children working on the invertebrates found in the school grounds may have the different tasks of using a branching data base for identification, adding information to a spreadsheet and producing a graph of data they have previously collected, using a floor robot to simulate the locomotion of different invertebrates and researching additional information from a CD-ROM. This type of lesson or sequence of lessons will require very careful planning and organisation.

- Only one group is doing science whilst the rest of the class work on other tasks. This type of organisation does not require high levels of resources and it is useful if the activity involves close adult supervision, for example, when complicated equipment such as a camcorder is used or if children need to go outside the classroom, although some activities can be undertaken by groups independently. It is relatively easy to monitor but time must be planned so that all the children can undertake the activity. You need to make sure that the activity is positioned to prevent the rest of the class becoming distracted or disturbed.

The science manager and ICT

The management of science at whole school level is a complex and skilful job. In broad terms it involves several key tasks including:

- advising others and disseminating information;
- managing resources;
- developing materials and documents;
- providing expertise and keeping up to date;
- liaising with others.

How these key functions include ICT for the benefit of the whole staff and the children in the school is of major importance to the effectiveness of the role of the science subject manager and involves them in policy decisions.

When science is taught well, resources are used appropriately, teachers are competent and confident in their teaching and enthusiastic about science, and know that they have someone who is expert in the subject to act as a reference point. With particular reference to ICT the science subject manger has to:

- consider how to optimise the use of ICT resources;
- ensure that the teachers in the school are confident about employing ICT in their science lessons;
- offer advice and be a source of inspiration;
- have an overview of the way in which ICT can be employed to maximise learning within science.

This means that the science manager has to consider where ICT resources can be used to greatest effect within the whole school scheme of work, the timing of each year group's work so that everyone does not want the same resources at the same time. It also involves the organisation of those resources so that they are available, in working order and booked out so that their location can be identified at any time.

Providing support and advice to the whole staff and individuals through in-service training, individual advice, disseminating good practice through bulletins, staff meetings or exemplar lessons will assist staff in having the confidence to make use of ICT within their science lessons.

The budget is also a key issue, not only in the amount of money available for resources but how it is allocated; for instance, will the ICT manager be responsible for all generic hardware and software?

Liaison with the ICT manager is obviously vital for the effective use of ICT within science and it will be important for the two managers to communicate on a regular basis so that they can work together to maximise the benefits of using ICT in primary science. It will be important for the two subject managers to identify and resolve issues that are pertinent to both. Some of these might be:

- Raising standards – how will ICT contribute to raising standards in science and vice versa?
- Staff training, awareness raising and communication of recent initiatives – how will this be achieved? Who is responsible?
- Resources – who maintains the ICT resources? Where will they be stored? Who is responsible for booking resources to year groups or individual teachers?
- Planning – how are the requirements of the National Curriculum for science and ICT to be met? Who is responsible for a scheme of work to include ICT in science? How will documents e.g. policies, schemes of work, long, medium and short term plans complement and support one another to ensure children receive a coherent programme for both subjects that provides continuity and progression?
- Budget – who is responsible for purchasing specific resources?
- CPD – what professional development do both managers require to maintain the needs of the whole school?
- Health and safety – how will specific issues be communicated to staff and children?

The ICT manager and science

The broad responsibilities of the ICT manager are similar to those of the science manager although the detail and focus will be different. There are two aspects to the role of ICT manager: to support and enhance ICT as a subject, and to support and enhance the use of ICT in the teaching and learning of other curriculum areas, including science. Thus effective communication will be a key determinant in success. Some pertinent issues which the two subject managers must resolve together have been outlined above and arrangements and lead responsibilities will differ between schools reflecting policy, expertise and ethos.

In addition to the issues already discussed, the ICT manager's responsibilities include:

- professional development, of a pedagogic and a technical nature, for teachers and teaching assistants;
- planning, ensuring continuity and progression of ICT knowledge, skills and understanding as well as for science;
- discussion with colleagues, including the evaluation of existing resources and the identification of needs and priorities for acquisitions;
- resourcing, including the location of hardware and software, access and booking and the provision of consumables (paper, printer cartridges);
- disseminating information on new acquisitions, on good practice and on useful sources such as professional associations, The Times Educational

Supplement Online, LEA and government advisory material;
- technical support, including problem-solving strategies for common issues, the effective reporting of faults, arranging repairs and maintenance;
- health and safety, for example the specific issues associated with using datalogging equipment in wet conditions such as the school pond;
- legal requirements – those associated with data protection were mentioned previously, and compliance with software licensing agreements.

Some primary schools now employ an ICT technician, who may have purely technical and resource responsibilities or who may be a teaching assistant specialising in ICT. In either case, whilst the ICT manager retains overall responsibility, the day to day delivery and management of technical support and resourcing may rest with the technician. Resourcing ICT in science is the focus of Chapter 6.

This chapter is designed to provide you with a range of starting points to find out more about the ICT resources available for use in primary science. It also includes further suggestions for their use in the primary science classroom.

Professional associations

There are a number of relevant teachers' professional associations, for science and ICT. These include the Association for Science Education (ASE), Micros and Primary Education (MAPE) and the Association for ICT in Education (ACITT). Each of these provide a range of resources, professional development opportunities such as conferences, communication opportunities and other support. Each has a website.

- ASE's extensive web site (www.ase.org.uk) includes resources for teachers, a technicians' area, an extensive bookshop and news of regional activities and conferences. Members receive *Primary Science Review*.

- MAPE's website (www.mape.org.uk) provides interactive resources and activities as well as curriculum support and advice. They produce three resource packs per year, detailing classroom activities, reviews of software and hardware, links to useful web sites and debates on current issues as well as a magazine and newsletter. There is an annual conference. A science resource pack (Focus on Science) was produced in Autumn 2000.

- ACITT (www.acitt.org.uk) produce a weekly email newsletter featuring ICT-related news, information on initiatives and projects, web site recommendations and technical explanations. There is also a termly journal, *Teaching ICT*, and conferences.

These organisations provide valuable support and resources and actively invite contributions from colleagues.

Software

Software suppliers
A few titles have been explicitly referred to in this book; this is merely scratching the surface of the quality material available. Suppliers of these titles are noted below.

Buying on approval
Software houses will be happy to provide catalogues. There are also wholesalers, such as REM (www.r-e-m.co.uk), who sell software and peripheral equipment from a variety of suppliers. Most software houses offer their titles on approval for between 10 and 28 days or so. This enables

you and your colleagues to evaluate a piece of software for yourselves and make informed decisions about spending limited resources.

Maximising value

Much of the software now available, both content-rich and generic, comes with activity ideas and plans. Sometimes this will be in the form of a handbook or manual, but often is contained within the application itself as part of the help and advice or teachers pages. The NumberMagic spreadsheet program (RM) for instance includes a range of prepared activities with full instructions. Such resources can reduce preparation time, can often be customised and are valuable in terms of demonstrating possibilities which may not have occurred to you.

Evaluation

It is important to evaluate software before purchasing and web sites before use.

Purpose. Is the content appropriate to learning objectives? Does it make use of the four functions of ICT (speed and automatic function, capacity and range, provisionality, interactivity)? Will it engage children?

Relevance. Is it designed for educational use? Is the quantity of information appropriate? Is it suitable for the ages and stages of attainment you have in mind? Does it facilitate differentiation? Does it provide feedback?

Interface and navigation. How is it organised? How long will it take to become familiar with the layout? What literacy demands does it make? Does it provide literacy support?

Accuracy. Are the contents accurate? Up-to-date? Free from bias?

Teacher support. Is there a manual or help file? Are there lesson and activity ideas? Are there links to websites with downloadable resources? Is there built-in monitoring and record keeping?

Technical robustness. How long does it take to load? How frequently does it crash?

There is a wide range of advice available to assist you in evaluating websites and content-rich software. BECTa have an easy-to-use evaluation form at www.becta.org.uk/technology/software/curriculum/evaluation1.html

Software reviews

BECTa have an educational software database at besd.becta.org.uk

Similarly, Teachers Evaluating Educational Multimedia (TEEM) have an extensive database of reviews of supplier information at www.teem.org.uk

Suppliers

ScienceFair, Bodywise, Plantwise (currently Acorn only), Sherston's Primary Clipart and StartWrite (to support emergent handwriting) from Sherston Software. See www.sherston.com

Textease (word processor) from Softease Ltd. See www.textease.com

Talking First Word (word processor) and NumberMagic (spreadsheet) from RM plc. See www.rmplc.net

Clicker4 and Clicker Grids including minibeasts (word processor/SEN support) from Crick Software Ltd. See www.cricksoft.com

Dazzle (graphics software) and Electricity and Magnetism: Primary from Granada Learning. See www.granadalearning.com

Counting Pictures, Counter, CounterPlus (graphing programs) and PictaPicture (database) from BlackCat Educational Software. See www.blackcatsoftware.com

Junior Insight (datalogging software) and Junior Pinpoint (flatfile database) from Longman Logotron. See www.logo.co.uk

FlexiTREE (branching tree database) from Flexible Software. See www.flexible.co.uk

Become a Human Body Explorer from Dorling Kindersley. See www.dk.com

Hardware

- BECTa produce a range of advice sheets which contain technical information, details of key issues, links to other sources and lists of suppliers for equipment such as *digital cameras, videoconferencing equipment and interactive whiteboards.* See www.becta.org.uk/technology/infosheets/index.html

- For more information about *datalogging*, including reviews of a range of equipment as well as activity ideas and resources see Roger Frost's Dataloggerama. See rogerfrost.com

- For more information about *Roamers* (floor robots), again including activity ideas and resources, see www.valiant-technology.com

- TAG Learning produce a *digital microscope*, among other resources. See www.taglearning.com

Video and audio material

The BBC and Channel 4 remain the key suppliers of quality materials. Each provides a catalogue each academic year, including programme notes and details of linked activities. Often the programmes are supported by a range of online materials for teachers and children. See www.bbc.co.uk and www.channel4.com

Internet resources

Grids for Learning
The NGfL provides a huge range of teaching and learning resources, as well as advice and information on issues as diverse as ethics and assessment. See www.ngfl.gov.uk

In addition, there are a growing number of community grids also providing excellent resources. The Northern Grid for Learning (www.northerngrid.org/home.htm) and Kent Grid for Learning (www.kent.gov.uk/learn.html) being examples. A full list can be found by searching the NGfL.

Government departments and agencies
The DfES (www.dfes.gov.uk/index.htm), QCA (www.qca.org.uk), Ofsted (www.ofsted.gov.uk), Virtual Teachers Centre (VTC) (vtc.ngfl.gov.uk)

and many other agencies and departments all have websites containing relevant statutory and advisory information.

British Educational Communications and Technology agency (BECTa).
BECTa is the key government agency for education and ICT. They have an extensive website, undertake a wide range of research and development projects and publish much valuable advisory material. See becta.org.uk

Focused searching
As previously discussed, searching for relevant websites can be a time-consuming business, but there are a number of focused searching environments relevant for teachers. These include the NGfL, VTC and BBC Education Webguide. The BBC pays teachers to research and recommend sites. Their webguide is a searchable database which includes the name, web address and a short commentary on the content. See www.bbc.co.uk/webguide/schools

The ASE and the Science Museum both have good lists of science links. See www.sciencemuseum.org.uk/education/index.asp

Safe searching
There are a number of search tools designed for children to use. These have a number of features to make them accessible for their audience and make use of various strategies to prevent children being exposed to unsuitable material. Ask Jeeves for Kids (www.ajkids.co.uk) includes an option for children to check their spelling. Yahooligans (www.yahooligans.com) operates a directory system.

School websites
A growing number of schools are sharing good quality resources with the wider community via their web sites. These include:

Sutton-on-Sea Primary (www.sutton.lincs.sch.uk);

Ambleside CE Primary (www.ambleside.schoolzone.co.uk/ambleweb/index.htm);

Snaith Primary (www.snaithprimary.eril.net).

Useful publications

British Educational Communications and Technology agency (1998) *Primarily IT: Using IT to Support English, Maths and Science at Key Stage 2.* Coventry: BECTa.

Bell, D. and Ritchie, R. (1999) *Towards Effective Subject Leadership in the Primary School*: Buckingham: Open University Press.

Davis, H., Frost, R. and Hemsley, K. (2000) *Science On-line: Practical Ideas for Using the World Wide Web.* Coventry: BECTa.

De Cicco, E., Farmer, M. and Hargrave, C. (1999) *Activities for Using the Internet in Primary Schools.* London: Kogan Page.

Farmer, M. and Farmer, G. (2000) *Supporting Information and Communications Technology: A Handbook for Those who Assist in Early Years Settings.* London: David Fulton.

Farrow, S. (1999) *The Really Useful Science Book: A Framework of Knowledge for Primary Teachers.* London: Falmer.

Frost, R. (1995) *IT in Primary Science.* Hatfield: ASE.

Johnsey, R., Peacock, G., Sharp J. and Wright, D. (2002) *Primary Science: Knowledge and Understanding.* Exeter: Learning Matters.

Lachs, V. (2000) *Making Multimedia in the Classroom: A Teachers' Guide.* London: Routledge Falmer.

Leask, M. and Meadows, J. (eds) (2000) *Teaching and Learning with ICT in the Primary School*, Chapter 6. London: Routledge Falmer.

McFarlane, A. (ed) (1997) *Information Technology and Authentic Learning: Realising the Potential of Computers in the Primary School*, Chapter 6: London: Routledge.

Monteith, M. (ed.) *IT for Learning Enhancement.* Bedford: Intellect Books.

Mosely D. and Higgins S. (1999) *Ways Forward with ICT: Effective Pedagogy Using ICT for Literacy and Numeracy in Primary Schools.* Newcastle: University of Newcastle Press.

Newton, L.D. and Newton, D.P. (1998) *Co-ordinating Science across the Primary School.* London: Falmer.

Peacock, G.A. (1999) *Teaching Science in Primary Schools: A Handbook of Lesson Plans, Knowledge and Teaching Methods.* London: Letts.

Sharp, J., Peacock, G., Johnsey, R., Simon, S. and Smith, R. (2002) *Primary Science: Teaching Theory and Practice.* Exeter: Learning Matters.

Sharp, J., Potter, J., Allen, J. and Loveless, A. (2002) *Primary ICT: Knowledge,*

Understanding and Practice. Exeter: Learning Matters.

Smith, H. (1999) *Opportunities for ICT in the Primary School*. Stoke-on-Trent: Trentham.

Somekh, B. and Davis, N. (ed.) (1997) *Using Information Technology Effectively in Teaching and Learning*. London: Routledge.

TTA (1999) *Using Information and Communications Technology to Meet Teaching Objectives in Science: Primary*. London: TTA.

Wenham, M. (1995) *Understanding Primary Science: Ideas, Concepts and Explorations*. London: Paul Chapman Publishing.

Wenham, M. (2001) *200 Science Investigations for Young Students; Practical Activities for Science 5–11*. London: Paul Chapman Publishing.

Smart Learning – ICT teachers books, photocopiable resource books and activity books for each primary year group, linked to QCA Scheme of Work for ICT. Tel: 01223 477550

Journals and magazines

Primary Science Review – Journal of the Association for Science Education

Teaching ICT – Journal of the Association for ICT in Education

MAPE magazine and newsletter – publications of Micros and Primary Education.

Data handling

Activities – Life processes and living things
- Sorting and grouping pictures of plants/animals.
- Comparing data sets to answer a question, e.g. does the largest minibeast have the most legs?
- Using data to compare and contrast organisms, e.g. number of legs and number of wings.
- Measuring and representing growth, e.g. cress or bean seedlings, sunflower plants, people, over different periods of time.
- Collecting and presenting data about the effects of a range of variables, e.g. light, water, temperatures, air on the growth of seedlings.
- Collecting data about the content and calorific value of different kinds of food.
- Investigating the effects of exercise, e.g. type of exercise, length of exercise time, pulse rate at different times after exercise.

Activities – Materials and their properties
- Preparing a database to group, classify and sort different types of materials on the basis of specific properties, e.g. solubility, effect of heating and cooling, electrical conductivity.
- Using databases to access information about soils and rocks from the local area and other locations.
- Preparing databases from first hand study of rocks and soils.
- Preparing a branching key of rocks and soils.

Activities – Physical processes
- Using spreadsheets to record data from investigations, e.g. the effect of different masses in a lorry travelling down a slope, the effects of different masses on springs, the nature of pendulum oscillations.
- Using data from investigations to present them graphically.
- Using data to predict and model the outcome to difficult or dangerous scenarios, e.g. the effect of very large masses on the length of a spring, the effect of very long strings on a pendulum swing.
- Collecting data on day length over a period of time and graphical presentation of diurnal changes during that time.

Sensors and datalogging

Activities – Life processes and living things
- Investigations about the effects of different environmental conditions in relation to the growth of plants, e.g. temperature, light, and humidity etc.
- Investigations about the habitats of invertebrates with regard to light, temperature, humidity, e.g. Where do woodlice like to live?
- Observing differences between members of a class, e.g. Who has the warmest hands? Who can catch the ruler the quickest? Who has the best hearing?

Activities – Materials and their properties

Investigating the properties of materials, for example:

- Which material makes the best ear defenders?
- Which material makes the best curtain to keep the sunshine out?
- Which material will keep my lunch driest?
- Which material will keep the ice cream frozen?
- Which material will keep the teacher's tea hot?
- How can we save the snowman?

Activities – Physical processes

- Investigating the effects of sounds as they move away from /towards the sensor.
  Which class is the noisiest?
  What part of the classroom is the noisiest?
- Investigating what happens as a light source is moved away from/ towards a sensor?
  What light sources produces the brightest light?
  How can we keep safe in the dark?
  What material is the most reflective?
  Which material makes the best sunglasses?
- Investigating the effects of heating and cooling.
  Will a large volume of water cool more slowly than a small volume?
  Monitoring the change in temperature of the classroom over one day.
  Which part of the classroom is the hottest?
  Does the temperature of the classroom vary if the day is sunny or cloudy?
  What happens to the temperature of ice/ice cream/frozen peas left in the classroom?

Simulation and modelling

Activities – Life processes and living things

- Exploring the functioning of the internal organs of the human body, e.g. the pumping of the heart, the growth and development of an embryo.
- Examining and investigating the effects of exercise on people of different levels of fitness.
- Exploring the structure of microorganisms and their pathogenic properties.
- Using adventure games to simulate specific conditions, e.g. no rain on crops, deciding how to irrigate land, send water to a town etc.
- Using data on a spreadsheet to simulate the effect of weight gain on an animal over a period of time if calorific intake is exceeded.

Activities – Materials and their properties

- Exploring the effects on particles during heating and cooling, change of state and dissolving.
- Examining volcanic reaction.
- Examining rock formation and structure.
- Exploring the events within the water cycle.

Activities – Physical processes
- Observing the effects of gravity on objects, e.g. a skydiver.
- Exploring and investigating different electrical circuits.
- Using data in a spreadsheet to predict outcomes of forces on an object, e.g. when a vessel will sink, when a spring will pass its elastic limit.

Control technology

Activities – Life processes and living things
- Programming floor or tabletop robots to imitate instructions provided visually.
- Using logo to 'pollinate' specific plants.

Activities – Physical processes
- Preparing programs to control a set of traffic lights, burglar alarm, a lighthouse etc.

Electronic information sources

Activities – Life processes and living things, Materials and their properties and physical processes
- Information and research.
- Posing questions and getting answers.
- Using interactive CDs for simulations and modelling.

Communications technology

Activities – Life processes and living things, Materials and their properties and physical processes
- Using a school intranet to share information.
- Emailing other children in schools across the country or world wide.
- Emailing scientists.

Publishing and presentation software

Activities – Life processes and living things, Materials and their properties and physical processes
- Creating report writing frames.
- Writing reports.
- Preparing displays and posters.
- Scanning photos – altering and editing for specific purpose, e.g. enlarging images of the surface of materials, the legs of a spider, the surface of a leaf etc to provide further information and insight about their structure.
- Using a keyboard overlay, e.g. to sequence the life cycle of a butterfly.
- Using a word bank or pictures etc to sort living and non-living, fruits etc, and to label diagrams, e.g. plants, electric circuits etc.

Video recording

- The growth of plants and use of time lapse feature.
- Nocturnal animal activity e.g. hamsters or badgers.
- Birds visiting areas in the school grounds.
- The changes to shadows formed during the day.
- Children answering questions in a survey.

Audio equipment

- Assessing children.
- Development and articulation of children's explanations of scientific ideas and concepts.

Overhead projectors

- Overlays.
- Presentations.
- Enlarged diagrams e.g. flower structure.

Cameras

- Pond life, plants, animals, habitats.
- Growth of plants or animals.
- Microorganisms.
- Materials including close ups.
- Materials in use, e.g. of houses locally or the school and its grounds.
- Phases of the Moon, planets and outer space.

Ball, S. (1999) 'How big is Uranus?' in *Primary Science Review*, 56, Jan/Feb.

BECTa (1998) *Multimedia Portables for Teachers Pilot: Full Report.* Coventry: BECTa.

Available at www.becta.org.uk/schools/portables/final/index.html

BECTa (2001a) *ImpaCT2: Emerging Findings from the Evaluation of the Impact of Information and Communications Technologies on Pupil Attainment.* London: DfES.

Available at www.becta.org.uk/impact2

BECTa (2001b) *Primary Schools of the Future – Achieving Today.* Coventry: BECTa.

Available at www.becta.org.uk

DfEE (1997) *Connecting the Learning Society.* London: DfEE.

DfEE/QCA (1999) *The National Curriculum: Handbook for Primary Teachers in England.* London: DfEE.

DfES (2001) *National Statistics Bulletin, Statistics of Education: Survey of ICT in Schools, England 2001,* Issue No 09/01. London: DfES. Available at www.dfes.gov.uk/statistics

DfES (2002) *Qualifying to Teach: Professional Standards for Qualified Teacher Status and Requirements for Initial Teacher Training.* London: DfES.

Frost, R. (1983) *The IT in Primary Science Book: A compendium of ideas for using IT and teaching science.* Hatfield: ASE.

Govier, H. (1995) 'Making Sense of Information Handling' in *Primary Science Review*, 40, December.

Ofsted (1999) *Primary Education: A Review of Primary Schools in English, 1994-1998.* London: The Stationery Office. Available at www.officialdocuments.co.uk/document/ofsted/

QCA (1998a) *A Scheme of Work for Key Stages 1 and 2: Science.* London: QCA.

QCA (1998b) *A Scheme of Work for Key Stages 1 and 2: ICT.* London: QCA.

Scaife, J. and Wellington, J. (1993) *Information Technology in Science and Technology Education.* Buckingham: Open University Press.

TTA (1999) *Using information and communications technology to meet teaching objectives in science: primary.* London: TTA.

Wegerif, R. and Dawes, L. *Encouraging Exploratory Talk Around Computers* in Monteith, M. (ed) (1998) *IT for Learning Enhancement.* Bedford: Intellect Books.

Willis, J. (1998) 'Data-logging isn't that difficult – and it can be fun' *in Primary Science Review*, 51, Jan/Feb.